Please renew/return this item by the last date shown.

So that your telephone call is charged at local rate,
please call the numbers as set out below:

	From Area codes 01923 or 0208:	From the rest of Herts:
Renewals:	01923 471373	01438 737373
Enquiries:	01923 471333	01438 737333
Minicom:	01923 471599	01438 737599

821
TRI

L32b

Please return this book
on or before the last
date shown or ask for
It to be renewed.

L32

11/12

2 0 NOV 1993

- 3 MAR 1995

- 5 OCT 1996

2 3 FEB 1999

2 4 MAR 2003

1 4 APR 2003

D1375908

JOHN TRIPP
SELECTED POEMS

Edited by John Ormond

SEREN BOOKS
*1989

SEREN BOOKS is the book imprint of
Poetry Wales Press Ltd.
Andmar House, Tondu Road, Bridgend,
Mid Glamorgan

British Library Cataloguing in Publication Data

Tripp, John 1927–1986
    John Tripp : selected poems.
    I. Title   II. Ormond, John, 1923–
    921'.914

    ISBN 0-90707476-97-X

Cover drawing of John Tripp by Richard Dean

*The publisher acknowledges the financial support of the
Welsh Arts Council*

Typeset in 10½ point Plantin
by Megaron, Cardiff
Printed by The Camelot Press plc, Southampton

CONTENTS

from THE PROVINCE OF BELIEF

from BUTE PARK

from THE INHERITANCE FILE

from COLLECTED POEMS

INTRODUCTION

Most of John Tripp's poems are variations upon elegy. They mourn a Wales oppressed by a still-continuing English infiltration and domination which have subdued, exploited and eroded the richnesses of Welsh tradition and potential, trammelling the past and poisoning the future. He mourns at the social entropy of modern life. His poetry presents the reader with a bleak vision that is never less than regretful and often bitter and angry. Anyone with a different view of things he decried as a "twittering optimist". I was among the many so labelled. There was in John Tripp's thesaurus only one worse term: that was "twittering thespian", his friend the actor Ray Smith excepted.

There was a core of melancholy in John Tripp's spirit which darkened his view of not only Wales but of the human dilemma generally. What joy could be plucked from a life which was doomed to be ended by the dehumanising outrage of death? Tormented and racked by what he observed of the world's condition and, too, by what he saw as the twentieth century's philistine refusal to accord the artist proper recognition and reward, he could burst into barely-controlled rages which would offend strangers and half-acquaintances, and try hard the patience of friends. These occasions arose during one of the many visitations of what the poet called his "Black Dog".

> I had planned
> a short break at the fair
>
> without spectre or phantom —
> a feast of affection.

I had hoarded my ration
of peace, of calm.

Then, edged at my vision,
the black shape loped;
a cloud slid down the side
of the green hill.

('The Black Dog')

At such times I'd tell him, "Don't talk to non-paid-up members of the Poets' Union". He was soon calling it the Sufferers' Union.

Only in love could any solace be found, love of a few dear and trusted women, and of friends whose companionship over beer could share his literary concerns.

John Tripp spoke outright in his own voice in his first small but important collection, *Diesel to Yesterday* in 1966. Eleven of the sixteen poems in *Diesel to Yesterday* are included in the present selection. Perhaps in its very title the poet encapsulated the essence of his unhappiness. When he returned to Cardiff from London in 1969 after working first as a sub-editor, and later as a press officer in the Indonesian Embassy, perhaps he was returning to Wales with a view of it softened by distance and by a nostalgia for a past made more beckoning by the isolation and cold comfort of London bed-sitters and greasy-spoon cafés.

He returned to his yesterday and found that despite an enlivening literary scene (the result mainly of Meic Stephens's founding of *Poetry Wales* and the Triskel Press which had published *Diesel to Yesterday*), the social fabric of the 'old Wales' was decaying, and this, too, was further cause to mourn. Worse for his pride, when the Arts Council grant — it was £350 — which had encouraged him to start as a free-lance writer ran out, he discovered that it

10

was difficult to make a living. His part-time literary editorship of the magazine *Planet* from 1973–79 gave him some respite. Otherwise it was a matter of small and occasional fees for poems, the rare commissioned article, the infrequent radio or television engagement and, most welcome, the odd poetry reading. The readings became more numerous and better-paid later on, but when circumstances bore in on him the "Black Dog" was soon at John Tripp's heel.

Then lack of company and a true comfort of his own — as distinct from his father's — home were corrosive and embittering. He gave me a sense of his feeling somewhat imprisoned. The warmth and generosity of his women friends (Fay Williams for some years after his return to Wales, and Jean Henderson for the last twelve years of his life) and the respect and affection of his younger contemporaries would bring him relief. Here it should be said that the poet had deep love and respect for his father Paul, a delightful and lively retired blacksmith, a man of Cornwall. Father and son got on easily. "There was a lot of old nonsense about John, but he was a houseful," the old man said in his loneliness after the poet's death. The proud plate *P. Tripp & Son, Farriers* was fixed at the side of the doorway of the bungalow called 'Pendarves' in Whitchurch. John was the son in the farrier's legend of that plaque. So what of this 'farrier's' craftsmanship?

His manner is direct and dramatic. Jeremy Hooker puts it well in an essay in his book *The Presence of the Past* when he says

> Language offers John Tripp less comfort than it offered Dylan Thomas. For Tripp is without a religion or a myth, and has no use for the symbols or metaphors by which harsh realities may be transcended and discords made harmonious in

another dimension.

John Tripp's words, while often full of compassion, are charged with the energy of pent-up emotions all of which are part of his mourning for his defiled 'yesterday' of Wales. When I got the feeling of the syllables, unhindered by any complex prosody, coming at me hard, I'd say "Johnnie, why not stop bowling bouncers for a bit and give us some slow left-arm spinners?" It was not his way but I was pleased to find among his papers something entitled 'Cricket at the National Library'.

> . . . I tried to oblige
> but the language cherry reared up
> again, wide of the off-stump.
> 'No ball' the umpire muttered. . . .

> . . . The atmosphere was quite
> heavy, good for medium pace as I sent it
> scattering the bails half-way
> to the sight-screen. My mind ached
> from the effort. 'That's better,'
> the captain said. 'You're coming on.'

In addition to selecting from John Tripp's various collections in preparing this volume I have had access to the poet's papers. These were assembled and broadly classified by Jean Henderson and I am indebted to her for the diligence with which she performed this task of love, for there were many hundreds of worksheets. Material from among these manuscripts is included in the last section of this book. I have included only poems which I think are up to the standards John Tripp set himself. Many of the work-sheets I set aside were earlier drafts of published poems, often much re-written. These make it clear that the poet worked hard at searching for the word that fitted his meaning. All the manuscript material is now deposited in the National Library of Wales.

In the last years of his life, though of course no one — least of all John — could have thought of them as such, the poet felt that he had finished his work. We'd sit with our pints in the Three Elms on Whitchurch Common and he'd say, "Giovanni, we've done it, all we could do. Now it's up to others." I protested that every writer felt like that from time to time, often for long periods, but that something new would come from somewhere. He did not believe it.

At such times I never sensed any great sadness in him; rather the quiet of a man who had eaten a sustaining if somewhat frugal meal at the table of life's joys. The joys he had savoured and treasured. In his last ten years he talked less and less, and then not at all, of the "Black Dog".

At the end of a party given in the garden of Dannie Abse's home in Ogmore, where the publishers of Dannie's new anthology *Wales in Verse* had been hosts, people were getting their things together to leave, drifting off to their cars, surfeited with good food and drink. Even the goldfish in the garden pool had had enough. John cajoled the caterers into halting the loading of their van and returned to the last straggle of guests with another armful of bottles and, "It's not over yet, it's not over yet". He meant more than the party, of course. For at bottom his philosophy (which nobody could dispute) was "None of us is going to get out of this alive".

He was a vivid and unforgettable man. Many who heard him read his poems will remember him. With his death Wales lost a devoted and passionate poet, and poetry itself a singular voice.

JOHN ORMOND

from
DIESEL TO YESTERDAY

The Diesel to Yesterday

There is downpour, always,
    as the carriages inch into Newport:
perhaps six times in ten years
    of a hundred visits to custom,
the entry to my country is uncurtained
    by rain or mist. I look
at the shambles of sidings and streets,
    the rust of progress and freight wagons,
the cracked façades of bingo cinemas.
    Sometimes I expect to see
the callous peaked caps and buttons
    of visa-checkers, cold sentries
on a foreign border, keeping out the bacillus
    in hammering rain and swirling fog.
Often I wish it were so, this frontier sealed
    at Chepstow, against frivolous incursion
from the tainting eastern zones.

Patience vanishes with frayed goodwill
    at the sight of the plump bundles
tumbling into Wales.
    They bring only their banknotes
and a petrol-stenched lust for scenery
    to shut in their kodaks,
packing out the albums of Jersey
    and the anthill beaches of the south.
They stand in line for pre-heated grease
    in the slums of crumbled resorts,
nose their long cars into pastureland
    and the hearts of ancient townships
that now are buried under chromium plate.

I catch myself out in error, feel
    ignoble in disdain.

The bad smell at my nostril
   is some odour from myself —
A modern who reeks of the museum,
   not wanting his own closed yesterday
but the day before that,
   the lost day before dignity went,
when all our borders were sealed.

Roots

I have thought about it, often in depth:
Wales is not simply a splodge off the map
of a tinsel continent, the far colony that Poles
or Frenchmen forget exists. It is not
even the accents of friends in the base capital
of a fat fool Tudor who signed the death pact
(urinating his satin with laughter
                as he slobbered venison on his whiskers).

It is more excitement's stab, as when
we once prepared for saplings' junkets.
It is the moment when the rain
falls at the border, as the winter express shrieks in;
it is the heart still racing, after all these years,
at the entry through night to the smashed south
of the small land that is mine
                     and like no other.

Soliloquy for Compatriots

We even have our own word for God
in a language nourished on hymn and psalm
as we clinched to our customs and habitats.
All those decades ago
in the chapels of the scarred zones,
lean clergymen made it quite clear
He had singled us out as his chosen.
He would care for the beaten Welsh people.
But now the strangers come to bang more nails
in the battered coffin of Wales.
                              Their sleek cars
slam up the passes and through the green vales,
the bramble shudders from the screaming exhausts.

A tangled image of pits and poverty,
Eisteddfodau and love on slag heaps
invades their haphazard minds.
Four hundred years of the King's writ
have not shaken their concept of our role: foxy, feckless,
articulate, mercurial, lyrical and wild,
we are clogged with feeling,
ranting preachers on the rebellious fronde.

All our princes gone, betrayal and sack
ended in a seal on parchment.
Our follies have all been almanacked, and our bards
are piping on reeds where once the trumpets sounded.
Death is the ancient popular topic we nibble.

Inept, they say, like the Irish
we have fought too long for the crumbs
from rich men's tables.
                              How could they know

for one moment of the steely wonder
of pride in legend in a sunken past,
the stiff stubborn strap to our backbone
that makes others still seek us out?

Lincoln, 1301

A divine slaps a small tin thing
on young Edward's skull, and so begins
the damp farce of royal yoke.
Now through thirty peculiar reigns,
chipped sculpted heads of monarchs
will fringe the roof of Llandaff;
chill charity of corpulent satraps,
wedged fat on their mouldy thrones,
will shut off tomorrow in this province
disputed since Caradoc's time.

The crown's lop-sided on the baffled lad
who will squat for twenty years

                       as king of nothing.
Think of the yards of parchment,
the drip of the red wax seals
to stream the keen expeditions out
        to collapse the Welsh!
But one generation dilutes its valour
into the next: soon the Fluellens flock
to Monmouth's banner, for a coin a day they are fodder
for a noble speech.

                As a nation sinks into torpor,
one heir is topped with the tin at Caernarfon
and motors to see dead Dowlais,
            with his lady back at the fort.
(His princely apparel crusts with dust
              in our bleak museum.)
Seven centuries distant from Lincoln,
in the swarming capital of the Welsh,
the latest incumbent is cheered
             on a rugby field!

The Incursions

Through marsh-locked border camps,
sheep on the spit and leeks in the pot,
the wind swept down from the ranges
as they took the full shock of the squadrons
                      galloping to their funerals.
Then scuttling across the fords like rats
came the carrion squeaking for thin spoils,
                      clamping on Dewi's back.

The heave of Saxon, Norse and Dane,
skill of the Norman, batter of Tudor ram
split the provinces with steel and knout
until the last of our princes sagged.

We wait on the punished parchlands
for the truth of Rhodri Mawr,
Hywel Dda or Rhys ap Gruffydd
to come bridging down to us,
               who are shrivelled by soft inconsequence.

Epitaph on our Military Defeats

Only the vaulted sky was witness
to that pillage. What hid in the hearts
of their captains, that they plundered thus?
What gain on gain could yet not stop
death's appetite? What catalogue of ruin
was needed to convince their kings?
On heath and beach the steel glittered
broad down a belt from Denbigh to the Vale
as a nation's breath was clogged.
Greed, the usurper of peace and union,
pitched its havoc into Wales,
slamming down the true credentials of men
                    quiet only in governorship.

Now at evening I watch the sun
burn slowly out, slashing its last streaked crimson
like that ancient blood on the western water.

At the Fords of the Teifi

Rain pelts in a screen
   on the landmark, the clouds scud
over unplaqued ground where the chronicles
   point to this blocking of conquest's tides
thudding in from the plunder bases,
   the stand on the western sedge
where Norman dropped with his Flemish link.
   The single alliance of dead soldiery
is scattered under Cardigan's turf.
   All our history then
was the sequel of burning keep,
   lost river, village and slope,
the old songs dying on the lips,
   and the old glint gone.

Rain slants down on the Teifi,
   grey ripples along the skyline
are the same on history's clock.
   The sea laps at Nefyn,
surges to Harlech and Borth.
   But no drum in the silence,
no flare to light them home.

In 1136, the Welsh under Gruffydd ap Rhys defeated the combined Norman-Flemish forces at the Fords of the Teifi.

A Parish

Those broken farms, the church brambled-over
and the parson wheezing his days out
before a decimated flock of the old
put this place on the rim of the world.
Another century creeps in the streets.
Like some looted abandoned village,
                        nothing stirs here.

I expect to see redcoats disappear
over the slope, drunk on loot.
The farrier, postmaster, saddler
hunch in the inn parlour
over dominoes. Their wives never come.
It is all very bleak, dull and deserted.
I hope they keep it this way.

Tragedy in Glamorgan

The blue and red are contending
for votes again in the rain. One is a colonel
of dead tanks, face pulped scarlet
and making noises about empire.
His thickness was bred under pith-helmets.
The other has crept from Shropshire,
knife-thin in concealed ambition,
with a shrew and three to support.
A third, the tired local man, sees inroads
into his land, the long taint
of glib promisers. He hoists
a kind tattered flag for race
and the logic of tidy backyards
far from the suave and the bland
manipulating fate like a card's turn.

The old listen close in the market place
under umbrellas. The young nod heads or shake them
or simply cuddle their darlings
as the third man whips through his story
of alien botch. The microphone crackles
on his last disgusted sentence.

The colonel struts, and the Shropshire lad
kisses the babies. The veneer of hypocrites
has yet to be scratched
while the shops still bulge and spill.

The third man is forfeit to his own ideal
and walks alone down the high street,
stooping in the rain to his cottage
where the air is clean.

Anglo-Welsh Testimony

We are not so different. Long parted
from the root, we are plain speakers
in quarters where eyes bulge at bluntness
or a nice turn of phrase. We reach for our pistols
only when we see the bigots coming.
Little gift for our native tongue
has not left us speechless
as we remind the governors that the governed
have souls. In the thick of parties
we become very Celt, disgusting the dull.
We often spoil functions, empty the rooms
with our preacher verve. Sensual,
we still appreciate a profile and a curve
vibrating nearby.

Exile is not treason to a homeland.
My suburb of Cardiff
(where they never say 'diolch')
is still on the line of the Taff;
Glamorgan clerk, Merioneth farm-hand
were in the same infantry waves.
At Twickenham a red-shirted jinking genius
still races the pulse; the huge choirs
induce a shiver up the spine.

It is true we have heard the English pound
whistling to us, and have answered.
But our small scattered talents
are all in the service of Wales —
each time our hosts recall the unusual,
when one of her sons triggered laughter
or brushed them inside their padded prisons
with the touch of old rare truths.

Exile

Much-thumbed in the good free library
that book of Auden's,
smudged pencil-stub on the margin:
'Glamorgan hid a life
          as grim as a tidal rock-pool's
          in its glove-shaped valleys.'

Chapel in the morning and prayers in the evening,
grace at table and the means-test fox
at the door, always starved, always
in a greasy mac.
The broth would be simmering, and the family
was one. Our house was seared by God
who would erect a stockade against woe, against
          the booby-trapped future.
Who would have guessed what assassins
lay in wait? The strumpet blonde, the gambling hellions,
the clawing temptation of ease
zooming into focus year by year
to dismember certitude.

And now, as the ice clinks in the tumbler, surrounded by
          friends,
one feels much cleverer, and lounges
in a blur of ethical indolence
on the long bent furlong of doubt.

from
THE LOSS OF ANCESTRY

The Loss of Ancestry

There is a blur at the border
    where once a straight line
cut clean as a knife.
    Ludlow overlaps Builth,
Gloucester spills onto Usk
    and Surrey is in Glamorgan.
The aim is a bank balance,
    automatic Jaguar and thirty-inch screen.
The capital without a theatre
    is full of hungry actors
and playwrights about to depart.
    The Queen's and the Royal and the Grand
heave with sportsmen;
    the only cultural arena
is the sacred turf in Arms Park.
    Cold the wind, and cold
the looming prospect
    as a nation cuts its roots.
                                History
that puts a great statesman in the same
    plane crash with a defecting bankrupt,
that brought the Welsh an English bible
    and forgets the names of its failures,
has no time for whimpered excuse.
    It neither cares nor feels
as we let what need not happen
    come to pass.

Three Imaginary Communications:

I. 'In the Matter of Penderyn'

'Merthyr Tydfil, winter 1831

We have hung one Dic Penderyn
twenty three years old
for involvement in riot
                 here in Tydfil.
The proofs were slender, sir,
as to his presence at all.
Now great crowds outside my window
follow his coffin.
             (Thus are martyrs made.)
We need Edward's Justices back,
a few turncoat hanging judges,
some Marcher lords and steel
to take these rascals' mind off
their damned Glendowers,
ap Gwilyms and God knows who.
Offa began a problem
            when he built his accursed dyke.
These Welsh will make the coronets rattle
at Windsor before they finish . . .'

Dic Penderyn led the riots in Merthyr in 1831 against the
harsh poor laws, and was executed at Cardiff Gaol.
Detachments of cavalry which were sent to the town were
disarmed and the rioters were quelled only by a considerable
military force.

II. Report from the Governor

'Caerffili, the tenth

I beseech you to consider
my relief. Half a year in this district
has ruined my health. I am going grey.
            You would not believe
the difficulties. These people behave
like apes. Only yesterday one flung a gobbet
of muck which hit my sleeve. It will take
generations to civilise them, for they ignore
our laws, we march them to church
but they hug their barbaric rituals
               in this language of theirs.
The magistrates have bulging assizes
and the hangman is overworked.
             In truth, it is hard
to govern this territory, and I would very much
like to return, with their dialect fading
on the road back to Ludlow.
           Meanwhile
I shall sit here and keep
control. My pennant just flutters over this roof.'

III. The Captain's Document

'Abergavenny garrison

As you ordered, I moved fresh troops
to scatter the foundry men.
One company was enough, no loss among us.
This is done. Six Welshmen shot dead
and several wounded. Some women and children
were hurt on the fringe.

                But now I must remark
my disfavour at the use of my toughs
for dispersing these people.
I formally declare my disfavour
before you now.

                Of no consequence, you say?
Who shall remember
one obscure captain of infantry in this land
doing his duty? You and I, sir,
will not even split a footnote
in history, our actions will fade
with the event. We will go out,
and this bad night in Monmouth
will vanish with the other nights
behind us and to come, will go like water
into sand. But tonight we solved nothing here
                       against this race.
They are not weasels.
One day we shall reap it,
our folly blown back on us.
They will turn, as proud people always turn
through the gun or through the ballot.
Mark this, sir, and remember it.'

On Mynydd Epynt

For miles no sign of life
but a few dotted families bent above the wheat
in grey patched cloth and shawls,
the children binding the stooks.
To the west a copse is blazing

and a barn burns beyond it. The commotion
disturbs the sheep and the peasants turn
from their crop at the drumming of hooves
behind them. Now the foreign troopers
ride again to depleted pockets

left over from the last rising. Cold gloved hands
tap saddles and wait for the signal,
their steel shines in the sun.
Those who are running now
out of the flames to the hedgerows

only believed in holding tight
to the place they were born in. Now come
these gallants who follow orders, and the home-sewn
ripped red dragon is thumped under hooves
into the raw grudging earth of Epynt.

This refers to the military clearances in Breconshire and on the
Herefordshire border in the 14th century.

Henry VIII, of Ignoble Memory

'In the wick of my heart,' he dribbled,
    'I have all love and zeal and honour
for these people.' Then he picked up a quill
    and signed the lethal bond,
stitching Wales into the cloth
    of his realm, before retiring to bed
with his queen of the year.

An old story:
    power two hundred miles off
puts out the flicker,
    sends in thugs who would finish
their grandmothers for a guinea;
    then come the converting priests
and the hucksters looking for plums.
    God knows how the language has survived.
A spider signature scrawled
    on parchment four hundred years back
sealed this barren marriage
    of incompatibles; the poor bride
was raped without consent.
    After our dynasties, after
the sabre squadrons and the marcher lords,
    a spoilt and randy king
joins the unjoinable.
    Up went this separate structure
of colonial loneliness —
    soon we were a limping stock
at the end of caring;
    even our own little jackals
scrabbled for the bones.

But some have the language still,
    and with others of England's tongue
couple arms in a spurt of the spirit
    that baffled fat Henry Tudor.

Requiem for Patriots

The last knots shuddered the dragon
ripped and torn on the wind's heights
against the three-leopard hordes
                        barrelling into freedom.
A buttress of collapsing flimsy
stood up to glory's dwarfs
slicing in waves on a new crusade
through pasture and crumbling settlement
for the folly of union.

Down the long tunnels propped with bone
lie the clanking knights,
all high and stupid on horseback,
behind them the pillaging pikemen,
merchants crawling from under the fungus,
and fawning purple clergy
waddling for God and Saint George.

Slow seep of alien taint
smothered the survivors' lines;
the sad bells sprinkled their cracked chimes
over the desolate townships.

'Saint Fagan Fight'

If you look close you will see
the chips in three-centuried walls
from a primitive fieldpiece
or sabre hacks in old trees.
                              Oliver's cavalry
flicked through those woods
on a day like this when the whole
countryside seemed afloat, the horses slithering
under skies running like wet mortar.

He was another, the sad protector,
laying more siege to us,
we crude objects caught in a joust
                              played out by England
for bishop or parson, for king
or Huntingdon squire. (Consider
the madness of that arrogance
when purple blood pumps through the veins
or Cromwells put on the cloak
                              of military messiahs,
their edicts pulping the innocent
like blows from musket butts.)

There was thin lard for us, as always.
The butter was royal, and the jam
went to the russet captains.
God knows what brought them
to these parts: pursuit or gain,
more lessons to be taught
to our long lovely line of unteachables
who went beneath their fields' lids
on a day such as this
                              in St Fagans,
the skyline thinning out to drab
watercolour, the drumcloud's grey drip.

Penyberth, 1936

Of all strokes, that was the one
to catch the breath. England's tin eagles
plonked a bombing run on the promontory of Lleyn,
consulting no other but the air lords
creaking down ministry corridors.
            The north Welsh settlers on the western tip
would again sit quiet under outrage,
carving their fields and muttering
at the rattle of lethal machines,
the twentieth century drumming
                              over their heads.
Bombs would crump in the waste lands
and all the scratching hamlets would tremble.

But then three men with petrol, and a box of Swan,
        put a torch to insult.
The empty camp blazed merrily.
Lewis, Williams, and Valentine the preacher
walked calmly down to the constable's
before his majesty's wrath fell upon them,
all the clanking legal gear of England
grinding into motion for revenge.
            A dim hung jury at high Caernarfon
dropped their brothers to the Old dead Bailey
where justice-lusting Saxons
whipped them sharp to the cells.

Did they see the flames from Pwllheli?
Did they see them from the capital?
Lewis, Williams, and Valentine
are not household names to conjure —
but thirty years past on a windy and distant peninsula,
these three stood up to be counted.

Meditation in a Time of Frivolity

An image is jammed in my head:
    it is dawn, hats with leek emblems stuck in them
lie in ditch mud,
    young men skewered and skulls smashed-in by butts.
It is Flint, Culloden, Connemara,
    wherever dead for the earth they lived on.
No hymns sung here, no plump massed choirs
    come down the mountain.

I find myself
    swung out to anger
beyond all causes.
    A piece of Lenin is in me,
wants gun-runners smuggled to Neyland,
    mortars on the roads to Ascot
and Goodwood — a Robespierre, a Danton thrown up,
    tumbrils creaking to plunderers' doors.

But what we do without barricades
    is to keep the steel within the will —
steely, cold and passionate,
    like sly grieved vixens.

Lloyd George

The cape and long silver mane
Like a retired medieval fencing master,
Standing on wagons in the rain
To push progress faster.

No dazzler was more a corkscrew
In the destiny situation.
Randy, too, in the cabinet rooms
When they foxed a whole generation.

For the Somme he paid the butcher's bill,
Saw marshals as craftsmen in crime,
Puffed on lusty to the end until
They buried the genius of his time.

Snap at Cold Knap 1938

The face I remember, and the name Vanessa.
Even through this mist she looks a rebel dresser.

Spain was a distant Bren-gun spit, young Auden unread.
We would cycle from the city with kissing ahead.

Kissing was the most that we dared do then.
The damp hulk of Bethesda loomed over her men.

We bounded to the sea in respectable rig.
But beneath my flannel the enemy was big.

Those days in heat like a mongrel dog
Panted to a close like some marathon slog.

She married into timber, Rolls at the door,
But the itch soon told her what lay in store.

Now she is split from her partner and brood,
The gin's tilted back, all her lovers are crude.

Family Supper

Back among them, the conversation
totters along local paths
that once brought yawns. Now
it is like common sense, I clutch to it.
After the ration of coldness
down in the smart zones, their warmth
spoons out in the price of clothes
at Morgan's, the toughness of joints,
Margaret pregnant and the baker dead.
It seems like a rope to cling to;
the ground beneath me is solid.

One aunt, a harmless sniper,
flings a blunt dart
at an absent niece. Her malice
is confined, part of filial games;
her gifts still go at Christmas.

Grouped over ham and pickles,
none here has heard of Pound
or Wittgenstein. With philosophy I fought
for years, but now the cutting edge
of argument is suet against their truth.
I believe in their quick kindness,
the timelessness of custom,
the simple plod of this remnant
that sees them through twenty weddings and griefs.

Matins

The flat blue days of summer
limp out, we wait for the russet carpets.
The last plane on the warm schedules
drops down to Rhoose, red lights flicking
from cockpit to tail. Friends behind glass
                              guide them in.
          South of Bonvilston
I sit on an old brick wall and roll a smoke —
the knots of vivid faces recede
and with them, too, their warped testaments.

I sit on till daybreak there.
Milk churns stand by gates like sentries
as if abandoned from an earlier time;
the land flattens down to the shoreline,
thin rain stipples the inland ponds,
farm sheds askew on a tilt.
Not a juke-box, not a stockbroker, for miles.

Narrative for Victims

It was never natural, sending them
cutting in the earth's gut
down shafts to the black roads.
Cheap coal bought the first Lagonda
and structures in Sussex, yachts to Nice;
it paid for pheasant and the warmth
a million guineas from Merthyr.
The owners drank penthouse cognac
far away. The pits gaped like wounds:
                              Britannia and Albion,
the blown Universal at Senghenydd,
Deep Navigation, Deep Dyffryn, Trelewis
vomitting half a century of filth
to sully these hills.
                    Our valiant could bend through the lifetimes
of punches in darkness. Each walk to the deep shifts
clocked them closer to death's whim.
                                    But in the wet
sudden week of grief's smash
the October slide on the pits' rim
dropped over our small generation.

Vulnerable's Lament

There is a magic
about Wales. If you do not see it,
I could not tell you. It is a magic
like the smell of the sea or the sight
of green hills, or of soldiers marching by.
It is a very old magic,
for Wales is an ancient and battered land,
yet the loveliest I know.
How can I write
impartially of a land that I love?

Rhuddlan's men
came over the mountains in the rain
and down into valleys to defeat. They knew that love.
All past and dead, all gone, like summer's futile wasps.
Their blood is filtered down to mine
perhaps one speck of it,
so unlikely, incongruous in me
who speaks sparse Welsh and wears a Cornish name.
I have no steel defence
against the jibe and easy mock.

Forgive me
who was born too late into Wales
and into this love . . .

from
THE PROVINCE OF BELIEF

The Seasons of Women

'Built different to us,' I was early told,
keep your smiles in reserve
and watch the dates. They are governed
                           by nobody's clock.
The hours of the calendar
move through the kick of birth, then on
through short prime to age's black fright,
the crow's-feet evening.
                           She is now
running with the tides again,
the phases of the moon,
no man's reason in this cold basic gap
will reach my kind animal.
Nature's wheel tows her to the sea's floor.
I learn to drill my own temper's ramp,
give way to her helpless whims,
my arms prop ready to guide her back in.

Homage to Aneurin Bevan

The last time the silver cascaded for me
was at Brentford, of all places. He walked
between two awed local agents
who revelled in short glory
with this paramount trapper of hypocrites,
this Welsh word-weaver famed for his coup de grâce.

No one knew then, it was near the end,
he was sick even then as we heard
him lunge at the ones who could never grasp
his gospel, at the clever who could handle
brilliance for a minute in the chamber
when he stayed on facts,
but were lost when he purred in the venom,
whipped when he launched the tirades.

The slight lisp was still there as he thundered,
drumming up compassion for the poor, still
boxing with the governors to take drabness
out of ill-favoured lives,
lifting his hand as if to snuff out a candle,
shocking us again with the unmatched wit,
the logic clear as glass.

It is easy to be brave in company, linking hands,
but this one was out on the ramparts, night after night,
alone. And when he disappeared,
a portcullis slammed down,
leaving the captain of archers outside.

Separation

But this night is the same
as any other night. The clocks bang.
It will pass like other nights,
while the squirrel twitches in his sleep,
the farmer sags bone-weary to his cot.

I will watch another sunset, clear and tangerine,
as cattle trail to their barns,
another dawn break through the west.
Somewhere the fox will stir in his loneliness,
a fieldmouse camp in an ancient boot.

If only we had been a simpler pair,
engaged in piecemeal tasks
on some outlying croft,
instead of the busy unimportant ones
everyone told us were correct.

Days will melt into days
when not even the shape of your hands
will be remembered,
not even the curve of the mouth
or the quiet sentences of disgust.

The lady in the shop still has her gout,
the neighbour hoses and hoses his car,
the tits land on the milk-tops,
the baker delivers one hovis and sliced.
Calamity on the radio does not touch us.

So I shall wait for more trains,
move from this point to that,
write you a last line about property.
I will observe it all as before
and wish we'd been simpler as the nights close in.

Death in the Family

(for my Father)

1. Tea and cigarettes

Pots and pots, packets and packets
   to smother these tensions of loss:
money can purchase a lessening of stress.
   The rooms were full of smoke
curling over twenty cups:
   we all sat around, inarticulate,
dumb in the silences.
   Neighbours called, cars came and went,
customary words were uttered.
   The very air stunned us.
None had a plan beyond their next cigarette,
   the next gulp of tea.
For the dazed who arrived from England
   and the filial nests of the valleys,
life was cut down to small movements,
   flattened by the mind's shock.
People stood up and walked about
   and then sat down again.
Newspapers were nonsense, a seaman's strike
   merely remote, unreal splotches on a page.
Only the whisky was missing: that false fortifier
   banned in our black Welsh rituals.
The hours were a series of images,
   memory flicking through abandoned albums.
All our brief triumphs lay pummelled by shock.

2. Officialdom

'Three layers are the same price as two,'
    the nice funeral-lady said,
nearly sincere in her forced efficiency.
    The technical details released us from thought:
there were forms to fill, grey men to meet
    to deposit one loving corpse,
to account for her sudden departure.
    (I felt like a sad errand boy
delivering back-payments to the grocer.)

3. Lament for a Maker

The civilised veneer of casket and hearse
    crawled to oblivion under sospan-lid skies;
the diggers scattered when the convoy came,
    the brown earth was piled up
as if waiting for a squad of troops,
    not one little woman;
the parson teetered on the grave's brink
    and spoke unheard consolations.

You went in June, that least vicious month
    of roses and visits, nothing
preparing you for the Adversary;
    your simplicity seemed eternal.
A cherry pie you cooked, and cakes
    were on plates where you left them
ten domestic hours before
    (when the Leveller came, he came quick).

The craft of your hands
    is on the lawn's borders,
your touch in every crevice of this house.
    You made friendships like dresses.
So sisterly to life, you slipped out
    unnoticed in sleep, the long party you loved
ending with dawn's embers in the grate.

Bewilderment now is my synonym for grief.
    Two miles away, three layers down you lie
at Pantmawr — my soft mother
    under the last of the wet blooms . . .

The Elders

They live in places
unpronounceable to most, caring like mothers
for speech, skilled turners on the lathe
of language, preservers of a truth.
In good company since Aneurin,
those acts of strange union did not break the clutch
through Cynwal, Llŷn and Prys,
Morris, Owen and Ifan
down time's ruin to their rooms
where they saved our page
                                    from the ashes.

These belong with the bards of free princes,
lightning cracking through the text
of praise for the sea and high hills,
framed by nobility of thought
and the heart's precision.

We who use the bricks of English
to buttress an old outer wall
dig hard for the roots of coherence
on the land our elders have built.

Honour to them, and their gnarled
stubborn craft for God and country.
For who loves not his own patch
of plundered soil, learns nothing of pity
                                    for all men.

Thoughts in Llandaff

Last night I heard the songs of fleas,
    hairy ones reciting their documents
of love: hot descriptions of armpits
    and the poor birds they took in the damp
back rooms of northern towns. Or thumping
    righteous and puffed against distant wars
that open no chink in their sleep.
    Somewhere between the mind and the utterance,
poetry lay gasping for breath.

    Now that seems far away. Below me
Byrd and Tallis soar through history's roof,
    above me the blue is soiled
by the trails of military jets.
    And behind me are the patched
family chronicles, all the coffins sunk
    from Tredegar to Penzance.

Children caper on the steps,
    their short innocence bolted in the best years;
on the lawns the schoolboys in red
    file to their future, and the old men
stump to their dusk.

    This ancient cathedral has stared
at eight centuries of children
    grown to connive at their own disaster —
the race for loot, the sword's argument,
    the blade up the sleeve, the mindless rifle's speech,
and the indifference in back rooms.

Yet through our chilled chronicles
I remember the kindnesses marked
   like fine pinpoints on a faulty map:
the friends who suddenly muster
   by our solitary tents,
and the rusted and priceless compass of love
   that will crutch us home . . .

Return

This time when the train pulled in,
my ticket wasn't torn in half.
I'd bought a single back to the beginning,
where people live at room temperature
and shopgirls call you 'love'.

I left nothing behind
but a series of rooms and landladies,
people with minds like cash registers
or index columns. I lost a hat in Hampton Court
and a box of books in Paddington.

I left nothing to remember
but memories in side streets,
faces that dissolve into calendars,
the glasses turned down
for those we never see again.

But why did I stay so long?
It was the indolence of the unplanned,
the belief that events would shape me
into contentment. How could I know
that my heart would speak a different truth?

An Elegy for England

In that old land the old men snore at Hove
as the bowlers swing from the sea end.
The sheep are straying in grass hedge-high
where the croquet mallets were lost.
Over the shires the streaks of scarlet
gallop for joy with their yapping packs.

The regiments of the line have been put to bed
with their colours and boots and Gatling guns;
the colonel stays on in the firelight
mopping his bread in the cold duck gravy
among the muskets and company silver.
He falls asleep on the crusty port,

dreaming of his military fudge.
Outside, the drunken bugler blows goodbye.
Where is the glory as old men sleep,
where are the rolls and rolls of honour,
their names in gold leaf and riddled with woodworm?
Where are the million black widows?

At Bath and Wells the people traipse
through glory to God and warfare.
The sun lights inches of dust on the battle pennants.
In public gardens the statues are spattered with droppings
and lavender pressed between leaves of books
hangs in the teashops of Cheltenham.

It is nice and easy in that country now
at the soft sweet end of empire.
                              The redcoats lie in Minden
and only the armies of the young
couple through the green parks.

Nelson's tunic is fading in Greenwich Museum
and his fleet's on the bottom of the cape.
England is quiet and silly and friendly,
banging a requiem march on a toy tin drum.

On My Fortieth Birthday

When I was forty the stocktaker came
to take stock. He was dressed in black
like that old advertisement for Sandeman's port.
Let me see your books, he said.
I blew the dust off my ledgers
and showed him the blank pages.
These are nothing but blank pages, he said.
Are you trying to be whimsical?
He had the flat voice that BBC announcers use
when they describe calamity.
My plans are still maturing, I said,
I am on the point of doing something important.
An old lady in Port Talbot likes two of my poems
and she's ordered two copies for the library.
I am piling my rubbish against oblivion,
stacking it against the dark.
If you go up to Aberystwyth
you'll find my name misspelt in the dust.

He looked at me in contempt
right through to the lack of backbone.
Yes, he said, but what have you done?
What have you actually done with your lovely life?
Well, I said, it's like this . . .
I groped for the cudgelled album
where the corpses were kept.

Outside was the switchyard, with the expresses
coming at one another from all directions.
I hadn't heard a bird around here for years.
Loneliness came down like a lid.

I'll be back, old Sandeman said,
you'd better get those pages filled . . .

End of a Farrier

The gangs of Irish in their huge boots
get up early. They have come here today
to destroy my father's forge.
Inside there is still the reek of burned hoof,
the rusted anvil is in the weed
with the punctured bellows. Dozers ram
the wood walls, the tin roof collapses
in a hung fog of black dust.

Hard on the slide-rule, the cranes swing and dip
hooking this shop of old craft off the map,
cleaving a furrow for the fast truck, Ford and Jaguar.
Here once the children stood for hours
wide-eyed at the hunter's kick, shod pony, shire
and the stunning palamino. Deep-voiced women
slid from expensive saddles, and men in pink
shared a flask before the blood hunt.

It is raining, but the Irish don't stop.
There's good money in wrecking
and the porter taps never run dry.

My father is handed a cheque
from the man in the bowler and grey suit.
He is now out to grass himself,
silently plotting to pack his gaping calendar.
We walk home in the rain,
away from forty years of his life.

The Province of Belief

Why it should be given
to this small land, this narrow sleeve like Israel,
to bury a secret,
            I do not know.
Yet it is there. As if somewhere
rooted out of two thousand years
the truth hides in the cracks
of chapels, in the tilted graves
stark on the evening skyline
above the decimated villages.
            (You would say
this place deserved better
if you knew of its disfiguring past.)

Here the kinder side of history
turned away, leaving these people
stranded on a tide of silver,
trudging to their bony faith,
keeping union with God's promise
of Caersalem beyond this dirt.
Here our hot little plans and appetites
buckle under the ruins of prayer,
far from the clanging townships
and the drag of the conveyor belts.
            Always through the clocking seasons
in Wales I clearly see
the botch of our desires,
the scrabbling rush to havoc
and the scratched yields of our lives
as the last sad threads of faith's remnant
unravel a glimpse of eternity.

from
BUTE PARK

In the National Museum

I went there on Tuesdays
at lunchtime, to look
at the Impressionists. Their colours
could take me into an old French summer
and let Cardiff sink in the Taff.
I never told her I went there
because she despised arty men.

Outside, at the top of the steps,
I took off my deerstalker
and hid my sandwich-tin behind a pillar.
Inside, under the big dome and high balcony,
there was dignity in the marble hush.
I adjusted my steel-rimmed specs
for the feast ahead. Then I saw the back of her
with an arm through some man's
going up the wide stairs. I turned back
to the revolving doors, scared,
thinking I would strangle her later.
She was wearing her best dress
and her hair was like flame.

Pantmawr

We came bunched from the mildewed tabernacle.
It was weather for the coast
and for lovers in parks.
The heat seeped through the glass
of our closed cars, shone black
and sinister as they crept
like sleek insects in our customs.
The driver and the undertaker
talked about sport:
I could hear them through the divider
and envied their detachment.
The sky clouded over,
the sun tried to pierce
the green triangle, weak rays slitting
over the flat ground. A thin wisp of smoke
spiralled up from a digger's compost.

We left the cars and walked
two by two down the lawn rim.
I wanted to run
the other way, but was hemmed
by convention. My father coughed
and the long line shuffled to the brink
as she was lowered into clay.

Public Library: Afternoon

An old man flicks pages of the *South Wales Echo*,
twenty students make notes for a future.
The pen folds in my fingers
like soggy felt, sweaty palms
leaking from love's tension
(much more of this palpitating risk
will raise my premium).
To live fifty years longer than Spinoza
and all the clergy of the heart
would be too short to solve this mess.
Wisdom in those shelves of books
is sponge against it.

She was met on the wrong date
in the wrong country. In the midwinter plod
we saw the comfort of courtship,
blind to the trigger-fine differences
that nibble to breakdown.
Life pays out enough rope
to hang its lovers.

The law says: no second chance this time.
                         To hermit-crabs
the dealer rightly chucks bad cards.

from

THE INHERITANCE FILE

Greetings, John Clare

In this bit of Northants
they locked you up for years
in a looney bin run by butchers
                  cold as a latrine.
You lived, if that's the word,
long enough to be an old man,
then they trundled you in a cart
back up the lanes to this
mossed grey stone among oaks
on a flat landscape of barley
with almshouses, Ebenezer chapel
and a couple of pubs.

I think you are the only ploughman
in English Literature. They say you shuffled
with one foot dragging in the furrow.
You were awkward and shy, with beauty
running in rhyme through your head.
At the museum your writing looks huge
and crazy, you were scared of everything
except woods and fields
                  and what you saw there.
For a while you were amusing to dukes;
in London you met Lamb and Hazlitt
whose carpentered prose showed up
your shocking grammar and spelling
which still made poetry like sapphires.

                  On the heath
ragged patches of burned-over grass
are littered with coke cans, chip bags
                  and spent sheaths.
The church clock fires off three in the afternoon.

We go mad, too,
but cunningly in quiet bursts
that explode under wrappings of sanity.

Greetings, John Clare . . .

Scott Fitzgerald in Hollywood

It wasn't this side of paradise.
The hooked mogul squinted at the script
and told him they couldn't shoot adjectives.
Neat gin was the solver in Beverley Hills
when the skids were greased.
He propped up the sham bar
in a place called the Garden of Allah,
framing those perfect sentences
that would never see the light of print.
His dazzle through the reckless Twenties
spluttered in a sink of pap.

The crack-up letters tell a story
of art bending to the wind:
a wife in long shock, a daughter scared,
the bad famine of his gift.
He felt that God might have kept
his shop open, or Lenin. He left
those chiselled fiction structures,
redeeming his evening of waste.
He died alone in the dream factory,
forgotten by most,
unfinished like his last tycoon.

Eugenio Montale

He doesn't say much.
If he did, he might say this:
'I am considered obscure.
Almost hermetic.
But no poet is cryptic
on purpose. Why should I write
merely to make a sense?
I try to find something
beyond words to convey,
I suppress any link
between image and idea
to let words go deeper
into meaning.

Life is a journey in the dazzling sun
along a wall. The top of this wall
is studded with jagged fragments of glass.
Do not expect from me
a magic wand, a miracle.
I can only tell you
what we are not,
what we do not want.'

from
COLLECTED POEMS

Letter from the Border

We are back here again
observing the poor clay and scree
of a foreign place, yet resigned
to this retreat across the Dyke.

Our faults were not named,
except that we loved to lament
a sagging culture. Dirge seemed fitting
when we looked at fossil and cromlech

or walked in the gutted vales.
Grubbing through yesterday,
we had a fickle crowd to please,
narrow as pins. Suave and bored,

some yawned at our plight.
We took the backward steps
to pierce the past, believing
it might shape the future.

I grant there was sentiment
in plenty, easy lumps in the throat
as we stood on abandoned quays.
It is difficult to praise a passing.

But gladly we go. The inhabitants
at last seemed brinked on hope.
Quite properly they brusquely unload
their mildewed chroniclers.

There is a time for elegists to depart
with their sack of nostalgia
and their dignity almost intact.
Change and continuity decree it.

Perhaps we bridge a gap,
reminding of old glory
to stiffen young pride. Perhaps
the toil was worthwhile.

We passed here once,
blowing a tin trumpet
or humming a sad tune.
Unmellowed, we raise our cups.

Caradoc Evans Revisited (1878–1945)

His invitations to tea were in a dwarf and spiky script
centred on three blocked inches of fat notepaper
with a list of his blasphemous works down the side.
In the stuffed house on Queens Square, among Buddhas
     and icons,
he lived with his bountiful wife, she veneered
by cosmetics, and swinging neck-length earrings.
He had a big nose and long upper lip, a face both bony and
     flabbed
with thin hanging skin, pouting mouth, hooded lids,
some shaggy goat's hair, and endless courtesy.
Together they made a fine pair of literary lions.

From Pantycroy farm he came, nestled in deep thrift
and close-handed rural ways. His sad teacher
used to cut off a piece of spanish, pop it in his mouth,
scratch his backside and say: 'There'll be whiskers on eggs
before the twelve times in your head'. Caradoc was a *twp*
with porridge in his bottomer's skull, fitted for nothing
but the haberdasher's barracks, forty pounds a year all
     found
with five hundred other serfs. Books came lurching at him
one by one, devoured in a room in Trollope's street
to take him from the reek of rolled cloth.

He dumped his frock-coat and pinstripes, galloping
from the button-buyer and the floorwalker. Soon his pen
was hacking in the gutter, let loose in Grub Street
until Genesis gave him a clue, until Marie Lloyd
taught him what to leave out. The style was hammered,
     forged,
but who would the victims be? Who would pay a slice
for those wasted years? His mind fondled the thought
of sweet grudge, his cutter fell sudden and swift

on his own people, on the peasants rooted to their dim west
        plot.
He knew the value of shock, that money-turner disguised
        as truth.

With sombre skill the mocker built his pillory and stocks,
jamming in the deacons' heads with pigmen, scullions and
        hags,
erecting a huge sty where nothing human could breathe,
where love disappeared under a hillock of dung.
Pity was stripped off, praise flung in the cowshed,
buckets of mud stuck on the ferret preacher and the joyless
        buffoon.
A biblical billhook rent through that ancient patch,
digging out the mange in corners, lopping at the mothball
        pulpits,
then pitching its flock like sheep on the barbed wire.
The grey spouter and the wicked shrew had received their
        Boswell.

Years turned, the scandalous narrative remained
        unforgiven,
its mellowed begetter nursing his sores and rusty sickle,
his inflammatory passage ending in spitting embers.
Now he wore black corduroy, magenta shirt, a cable-stich
cricket sweater over an old decaying frame.
Under his brimless straw hat he puffed on a pipe,
the drooped eyes and huge beak still gazing and sniffing
at a charmless world, out of a gnarled and scooped face.
Then on a cold winter's day he went, this dazzling prodigal
unique in his gift and supreme in his venom.

His art was blunt inside its shattering glove,
his spleen well thrust against a failure of heart.

86

He offered no quarter to the grubbing merchants of cant.
But did his scarecrow vision of flesh and spirit,
his flapping arms that terrified the crows of sin,
ever let in a glimpse of golden cornland?

In Memory of Idris Davies

(for Glyn Jones)

He was short and sturdy, one of dim Picton's Silurians —
dark, tough, stocky, thick-necked and durable,
bantam of a race that went down before the blond Celts,
then packed the pits and Big Seats and choirs and scrums.
When you saw him in a drizzle on the Capitol steps
he wore a cloth cap, wool muffler, gloves and brown mac
with old wire specs askew, mended on wet-look solder,
one pebble-lens flattened tight to the eyeball.
He held his collier's Woodbine in the cup of his wounded
    hand,
easy and serene, without sulk or boiling mouth.

Rhymney and poverty made him. He was haunted to the
    very end
by the skull of want and the furious gospel
lashed from the radical pulpits. Green dawns of childhood
by the river and black alp, dust-hung summer afternoons
among nettles in the pityard with the lost ragged boys
led him and them to the customary crawl
under the earth, along the seams of Gwent,
thin layer of grime washed off into the evening tub.
Then the long lonely track to shape himself,
the bitter chronicle beginning to itch inside his mind.

Out of such parched soil, such pitiless rock
his harsh plant grew. No document was ever carved before
from this slab of ferocity and love —
a wept lament for all those diggers in the dark
and their broken kin, abandoned in the tunnels of the
    south,
a testament of disgust drilled at the core of wrong.

He never served an image of moonlit brooks
or salmon-running streams, or blue remembered hills.
His was a bedded landscape of human figures
bent but proud before a random wind.

Memory must have plagued him like a pox
as his exiled heart was shuttled about England,
as honesty tested his acceptance
through the soft quilted ease of Bohemia.
In the staff-rooms of mouldering schools,
what remark could have triggered a vision
that shot him straight back to his bleakest ridge?
In those gay nights of bellowing talk,
did the turnkey suddenly slide in his greasy coat
to show him the ramshackle beauty of Wales?

Stripped, bare, stark and pure the lyrics come,
hard and lovely as the place that formed him,
true as the tribute to his ravaged land.
His goodness seeps down the years to remind us
of faith to be kept in the ruins. His last limp
over the mountain road, his suit hung loose on the frail
        bones,
will take him south again to the buttercup fields,
to the dream in the vale when he was young.
Your sad bells of Rhymney ring sweet and clear, Idris,
and the pigeons are homing. They are coming home.

Diesel '75

It is sleeting at Newport
   when we pull in. Does the sun
ever wink off these roofs,
   warmth smuggle into the streets?
Victorian slabs of granite
   conceal the warrens,
and canopies of slate
   hide the twilight rush.
The border remains unsealed,
   wide open to the future.

I watch them tote their travel-bags.
   Still they come, the snappers
of lake and ruin, festooned
   with exposure-meters,
and Kodachrome in their pockets.
   They are just like us, abroad.
Am I mellowing, that I cease
   to care? Or could this be
the end of our anger
   as a province lifts its head?

The Last Picture Show

They pulled down the Tivoli
this morning. Too long ago
I was fixed to its jigging screen
as Scarface unlocked his Thompson
or the Seventh Cavalry charged;
as Tyrone Power and Basil Rathbone
fought to the death in 'Zorro'.
The actress most to be avoided
was Shirley Temple, and other syrup.
I couldn't believe in heroes,
but the villains I understood
with their clear, uncomplicated aims.

The old man in the box
collapsed after running 'Dawn Patrol'
for six weeks. I took him
apples and tobacco at the Infirmary
with a jovial card from the boys.
He's gone now, and so is the owner
who allowed us to smoke. Today
my steps led again to the cockpit
where so much time was spent in the dark.
I looked at the grey dust hanging
above the rubble, and some reels of film
trapping Alan Ladd and Bogart forever.

Threnody for the Governors

Unaware of their singular talent
for woe, there was a hole
where a moral core should be,
some helpless streak
of pride, secure as princes
within a king's gift.
A sense of mission trotted
orderly across the border.

First, in muddy sheepskin
with blades, disguised as valiants;
then later in brougham and frockcoat
with houses in parks,
long lawns, flunkeys at the door
tea and love behind french windows —
but settling on us, steel knuckles
inside a soft glove. They nurtured
a colony spewing minerals; seeded
fresh stock for dominion
compact in turreted manors
now open to the bats, generations of moths
eating the tapestry.

Not one of them proved
their pattern right, as we stared
at each other across barbed wire.
        In the ditch of history
the truce papers wilted
waiting for the signatures —
both sides under shadow
of their own scythe . . .

Defence of the West

1. Castlemartin

The long Panzer huts were deserted,
some windows and a chimney smashed.
Soon thistle, nettle and weed
would win back the ranges.
Farmers stumped again through mud,
tractors jerked forward in lines
like peaceful tanks, and sheep
safely grazed. An occasional bang
was the last of the shots out to sea
to use up the shells. I forgot
why they came to this place.

Their markers and targets
were rusted and sodden by rain,
the crossings greasy from track-oil.
Hooded against the blast off the sea
I heard a gun thump, then a short
gutteral command. Red flags drooped,
Achtung said a tilted board
and overhead
the last chopper went for a joy ride...

2. HMS Felicity in Fishguard

    'We have the most
sophisticated gear,' the captain said.
    'Can I see it?'
               'No.'

'Why not?'
        'It's secret.'
'What do you aim at?'
           'Towed targets.'

She sat in the bay
a frigate of deadly science
that could blow old Fishguard
into the water. The captain's
voice was royal yacht squadron,
his intelligence as crisp as his white
shirt; in blue cummerbund and black
dancing pumps, he gave me
pink gin in the teak wardroom
and produced his handsome young officers
who were ready for World War III
('We could put up a pretty good show,'
a rosy-cheeked boy said to me).

Layers of steel hid technology
that could pinpoint a raft,
knock out a port miles away.
We chugged back to the quay in a launch,
and by dawn Felicity had gone
to shoot missiles at floating planks.

3. Interceptors over Gwynedd

Talking to the shepherd, my eyes
kept on his ginger stubble
and a Woodbine jammed in a hole
in his upper teeth

94

(it's not often you meet someone who can do that).
He scratched the dog with his stick.
My boots slithered in the muck,
it was cold and his breath plumed
as he spoke of sheep and weather
with the nous of centuries behind him.

At first it was a far-off buzz, a sort of
hiss. 'Here they come,' he said.
We stopped talking and listened.
Then out of the west beyond a lattice
of trees, pummelling the ground,
came the hunters suddenly above us
screaming as they bullet-streaked
across the morning sky —
slide-rule perfection in itself
headed out to Menai and the sea.

Two swept over, then one, sluggish
like a slower younger son
still testing its speed; you could see
red-and-white dicing on the nose.
In seconds they had gone
and the trees stopped shaking;
the silence was full of vibrations.

I looked from the sky
to the shepherd, his thin face nutbrown
from years of coastal wind, a weak smile
seaming it as he glanced around the fields.
'They were shifting,' I said.
He lowered the fag to his bottom lip.
'That's progress for you,' he said.

Concerns

Such small ones, when I consider
the weight on family men
of carrying theirs.
Today, for instance, will see me
caring for an elderly aunt
who is visiting.
She is slow and deaf,
but proud and stubborn.
I would not reveal my concern
openly to her, yet I feel
we may not see her again.
I shall arrange a surprise
before she goes: a choice
of my late mother's millinery
and a sherry at the Park.
I wish my father could return
on the west train with her
to see Cornwall again.
He has lived here long,
but his home is there
and always has been.

I carry no pack on my back
and the days look smooth
in others' eyes. But these
small matters wrapped in silence,
these responsibilities of pity
can vex and nag. They seem
suitable candidates for concern.

A David Jones Mural at Llanthony

(for Jeremy Hooker)

I

Rain had turned the countryside
into a sump. From Capel-y-ffin
that constant, dripping screen obscured the hills,
drowning a file of ramblers
and swallowing two sad pony-treks.
I sheltered under sopping oaks,
then lifted a latch into a long
monks' larder, with boxes of bad apples, oranges,
mouldy biscuits and cake,
a mysterious pyramid of fresh eggs.
On the stone lay a splintered carafe
crusting a sediment of wine at the base.

Then I saw it . . .

Delighted, I remember thinking:
if the dealers receive wind of this
they'll climb here with mallets and chisels.
It was a signed
original, flaking fast on a cracked wall —
the dark buff and faded red of his fine
leaning script, the numerals of Rome,
a Christian head and a believer's praise embedded in the
        text.
Time and neglect were chipping at beauty, scraping a
masterpiece.

(He had walked this corridor,
studied the portraits of Tudor martyrs,
put his brushes on the floor beside me,

97

and gazed at the Black Mountains.
A few days, fifty years before,
occupied his mind and hand
to leave us a lost symbol
like some flourish of hope.
        Feeling, wondering, testing, watching,
        seeing clues in fragments —
        'For it is easy to miss Him
                at the turn of a civilisation'.)

II

Six winters from the Flanders mud
he came here, looking for a slot
of peace, some method to preserve sanity.
Deep reticence after misadventure
informed his plan; the chronicles that unlocked his horror
were yet to be written.
                        All that complexity,
the full bulging yield of myth
was growing as he painted on a monastery wall —
history to be sacked, language to be made,
the honours far off, and the life
continuing, aimed at the past.
Its price brought the long
loneliness, to be lived through in a Harrow room,
for one soldier of goodness and truth.

The Icicles of Grief

— Well, that's that, my grandfather said.
The horses kicked up the slush
as the wagon pointed lifewards
again, back into the charades.
Traps bumped a score of kin
over wheel-ruts and potholes
to the house for sandwiches and tea.
Grandad took a swig from his flask.

Two miles away the old lady was bedded
after fifty years of dominion,
settled beneath a hedge of nettles
not far from the Ogilvy pit.

To me the matriarch was a ramrod
in bombazine, unsmiling always,
as if in perpetual mourning herself —
a source of acid-drops and pennies.

Probably, it would take a week
for this loss of the familiar
to sink in. There was a drill
here, the discipline of dry eyes.

Later I would learn to hear
the thunder of reserve, come to know
our squirm at the mention of death.
But that day I was unprepared.

Now, flicked through our blank ritual,
the horses clopped to the entry
in a flurry of snow and the veils
lifting from the white faces.

Such restraint, I remember, their lips
sewn. Not a solitary tear
dabbed by the women as they glided
in whispers, and the sheepish men
anxious to be gone. How odd,
I thought even then, that soon we slip
back under our masks, and button-up tight
our pain behind the black apparel.

Headmaster

Now, thirty years on, I shift
nervously in respect, perhaps slur
my speech on the tavern court.
He is still formidable.

Under his arm is the fat
original Gibbon in faded red boards,
savoured with a wall-length stock
at his widower's villa.

He has a stick, and his limbs
are frailed and bent, but the awed clock
could stop in his Star Chamber
long back when he told me

I could amount to something, or
nothing. How many callow bluecoats
passed his window into the grey
mixer beyond? He saw them run

towards it, without literature
or history. Sometimes I think
his kind of iced wisdom is best —
the goodness of sad reason.

Fidgeting there, trying hard to account
for the locust, my chronicle bulges
to impress him. As I skulk off,
his example makes it seem nothing.

At Bosherston Ponds

In November it is desolate, and distant
from the ruck of summer. The mashed carpet of leaves
lie apple-rust in the gravegaps,
their season done. Waves of high grass
wash about the church, drowning
the sunk mounds, the lopsided slabs
askew from weather and dying stock.
Names illegible beneath layered moss
clip me to futility, yet give that mild
pleasure we feel in cemeteries.
I am cousined to them by nothing
but a moment in Wales
and the loom of skulled union
under roof of turf with the winning maggot.
History on this dot of the map
is sufficient to make me limp
a foot high. In my pocket a poem
shrivels to pinpoint. I look backward
for the peglegs hobbling
while I walk in cold time. I slither down
a long path mucked to a whirl of dung
and hang onto branches for support.
                              Solitary now
on a balsa bridge across the lily ponds,
I lose all strut.
Skidding along slotted planks, the bridge shakes
as my flimsy tenure shakes. I look out
at sheer rock and sloped dune, stretches
of water lily: something perfect occurred here
long ago, hacked in silence
without men or words — gaunt-winter-perfect
in frame of steel . . .

                    I turn back
up the steep track of churned cattle mud
where dead anglers trod, full of their hooked skill,
and riders stumbled, chasing a streak of vermin.
                    I scramble up
to slap of sea wind in my face
howling through the lost cemetery.
To the bang of winter, the coming events
and the illusion of action.

Near the ancient village of Bosherston on the South Pembroke
coast, the lily ponds are so old that no one has been able to fix
the date of their forming.

Notes on the Way to the Block

There's a good crowd here today
to see me off.
I never knew I had so many friends
or enemies. I see several
familiar faces, and breasts.
There's one *cariad* smiling
whose knickers I took off
long ago in West Tredegar.
I don't see anyone crying.

Well, now to get down
off this bloody cart.
A few in the crowd
give me a helping hand,
eager to speed my departure.
Nice of them. I never knew
I had so many friends.

The sun is shining
but the birds have gone.
Birds can sense a bad scene.
The crowd is silent, a bit awed
but looking forward to the experience.
I mount the steps, alone,
see from the corner of my eye
the executioner approach
wearing a jester's cap and bells.
Good. We don't want black
or melancholy at a time like this.

His axe looks sharp.
I give him a cigar to make it clean and quick.
Don't I get a last request
like a joint or a slug of whisky?

Someone in the crowd giggles,
but I can hear one woman weeping.
I take a last look at the sky.

Tomcat

While others were curled on their evening rugs
or purring on laps to a loving stroke,
this one was loosening dustbin-lids
to get at the fish-heads. With a rattle and crash
he'd dive in to select the garbage.

We say we like cats for their coldness,
seeing in their chill the slow dignity
we wish we possessed — no messy affection there,
nothing of slop to bring a rift
between Tom and his lessons in reality.

We had a blackbird family in a laurel hedge.
He waited on the wall for treacherous dusk,
squeezed through the branches and murdered the mother
and chicks. We saw the red feathered remnant, scattered
in a raging minute from life to gobbling death.

Those like him that lope in predatory dark
are men's men, criminals looting on the run.
If they see a hot cat on a roof, sex is the second choice
to a guzzling kill. His ancestors lived on farms,
the equal of anything vicious on four fast legs.

His history was probably short, a panther thrown out
from a series of heaving litters
stinking in a barnyard of cat orgy —
his mother and brothers drowned in a shuttered barrel.
Flung in a ditch, he began with grass-high vision.

He stared at the battlefield, grew bigger on mouse and
            sparrow,
checked the competition and liked what he saw.
No pamper of milk came to soften him,

human hands were to spit and bite at.
When he arrived in our garden, his pessimism was quite
        complete.

No one ever called him pussy, except old ladies
fuddled in sentiment. A black scavenging scrag,
for a month he shocked birds from the lanes,
rummaging wherever a stench was pleasing
and lodging on a sack in a shed.

There they found him, asleep, and clubbed him to a pulp.
He wouldn't taste full cream now, or caviare from tins.
Lean aloof prowler, he deserved no catafalque.
But after they threw him in a pit, I put him on a spade
and buried him under a scarecrow hanging in the wind.

Welsh Terrier

(for Fay)

Taffy of course. He *would* be called that,
our family being dangerously original.
He came as a mischievous black-and-tan ruff
from some Vale farm, affection leaking from him
in a coddling house. We had our work cut out
keeping him within his breed's toughness,
this ancient hunter of otter and fox.

Above the spoiling he kept himself hard,
brave in terrible scuffles with vicious strays
resentful of his clean line, dark vindictive curs
with wolf fangs. Scars and stitches grooved
his wire-wool head. With brisk rump and back legs
firm against attack, his great humorous whiskers
grinned at a world full of romp and forage.

Sometimes, over the shagged mountain
for three days he was missing on a bitch
jubilee. These roaming strumpets liked him
for his talent of tenacious pursuit
and rough satisfaction. In the mud lanes and farms
around Rudry and Machen, a few mongrels still trot
the wide district of their father's pleasure.

As he grew older his timing went, the small body
a lumbering cart, feeling the January edge
in bitter snowfields. Not even he, old loyal bruiser,
grizzled on twinge and cramp of age,
was fit to see the light of day. We
trickled brandy into him and mopped
his dry mouth with a cloth for a week.

We only heard him growl once, like an old man,
when his last ruined blanket was removed.

Airfield

Flung down between useless scrub and good farm marl,
it sits there like some patrician folly
nobody wants, unmarked on maps,
with one riddled windsock, dented oil-drums and a few
rotted chocks, old sand seeping from bags
on the gun emplacements. Foul-stench Nissens
shudder in the whistling gusts, are for lovers
displaced at night, and the snouting
weasel, stoat and rat.
Invincible nettle and weed are cracking
the concrete open, a sagging hangar
rattles under shreds of camouflage net.

Seeing it, I think of the brash squadrons
bundled off to their dates
in that jubilee of turbulence,
the posthumous gongs and citations
for an élite of valorous wings.
Would I be here but for that kind
of fealty to a striped flag
blasting the Breton pens and Baltic
rocket shops in a cortège of wrecked metal?
Who now in this cenotaph silence
can give them a late benediction,
or say the last paternoster?

Famous Man

The devoted plasterer and his mate
on a plank between two ladders
fixed the blue plaque to a wall.
It tells me that he lived there
and gives the dates of his span.

What it doesn't tell me is where
he was born, the narrow street
that put pity and steel into him
in equal quantities. The tub-thumper
drumming up support for justice,

mesmerising the poor on corners
and bulleting through the council
to Westminster. How the people
loved him, and would have followed
his mind and his heart to millennium.

The proud plaque of Wedgwood blue
doesn't say how he spent
too many hours in turncoat lobbies,
in dark-suited trimming clubs
or in week-end boxes by the river

where love of the game for its own sake
is all. Why his soul got crusted
with shit on the long way up
and the short way down. And what happened
after power riddled him like pox.

Dewi Emrys

Vagabond with a taste for wine and people,
he took four Chairs and a Crown,
then pawned the Crown in Swansea for a couple of notes.
He slept under paper on the beggars' benches
and in Cardigan barns, glad of a crust of bread
or a ladle from the churn. On street corners
through a screen of rain you might see him
hitch up his collar below the dripping troughs.

He should have been a cocky troubadour
stepping from tavern to tavern
with his slung lute, singing for his supper.
Our century could find no home for his heart.
What trouble takes a man of skill and vision
to the skidding edge? A wayfarer like all of us
but haunted, he journeyed from a warm centre
high in the bright pavilion of bards

to the lost shabby rim.
I think of him when he was alone
with only a pen and a gaping page,
facing an old language with humility,
testing the sounds, turning and turning the lines,
drumming their response through his head.
He sits with Dylan in that narrow room
where the lyric is measured, sealed and folded

into itself, where the craft is always stubborn.
I saw him once in a smoky distance
outside his nest at Talgarreg, sweeping the leaves.
He wore an old fisherman's hat and a leather jerkin,
seeming peaceful at last within that silent frame.
The moss is over him now, the briar and ivy.

His mark is a perfect quill and a brimming jug,
a short poem shaped like a heart.

The Gnarled Bard Undergoes Fame

1

It is laughable really: three decades
of drought, pie-crust flung to me
like a dog at the metropolitan feast.
Behind shutters in the damp west
I weaved patchwork that resembled vision.

Now the rodneys come, to a hermit-crab with pad and
       ballpoint,
contraptions to frame my expression
and every move, supposing my cracked lips
utter truth or a white panacea.
They chase rainbows through my skull.

Wine is flowed for me, with rump beef
in the best crumbling hotel: suddenly
the landlord looks up, greasing his finger
for something he doesn't comprehend.
England brings glamour with her queens.

Clanking, ferocious in winter doldrum,
I manage a stiletto smile for the scribbling
beaver, a few icicles of logic
hissed at the modish don.
They lap it up like cats on the cream.

Perhaps they lick some prospect
of farce, my joining the cram of explosive
wit, with the lyrical child who died
in the heartless skyscrapers. But I am not
given to splendour, my brief is spare.

Wales bleats through its sheep in the corners
of sodden fields, their sackcloth shepherd
limps home to his tumbledown wreck. How
can I tell these shiny gropers of the long
fortitude that went to our making?
(Ancient fuss, the reason may be on their side
as the globe shrivels. Engines drum
above me, on their way to slicing
the barriers. Europe looms like a fat egg.
Yet still I walk to the sheep's pasture.)

The young sometimes stroll to my boots
with dignity, holding their own crimson banner
aloft. Scags of longing for ripeness
rip my album, my old chronicle wilts
under heat of enterprise.
Slip back the thread a notch or two
and the rust shows. Between country, love,
and the grasp of a psalm, slow pillage
loots the soul. Now the rodneys slide
through my bramble for a heavenly word.

I could hobble to the rim of this province
and jump off, my loneliness and I
sinking among the silent fish.
But I shall wait for tomorrow, when the noise
has gone, and I may listen again to the wind.

Turner in Old Age

I

Remote, cantankerous and fat
little man, hermit-mossed and solitary,
he slipped all the hollow connections
his fame could have brought.

Odd shylock in retreat, his bleak ways
spread rumour of madness.
At Chelsea he locked his spirit
behind the screen of his landlady.

Praise was heaped, yet he festered
at those barbs of 'suds and whitewash',
the dauber with a dripping brush
soaked in a bucket of ochre.

Puny man was swallowed by his canvas,
crumpling before nature, the brief split-
second of his span dissolving
against time, and its companion, light:

Yellow flame at morning, crimson
shockbursts of noon, an orange glow
sunk behind a ruined city;
rainbow shafts flooding through glass.

What he glimpsed was a passing
of empire, vainglorious shreds
at sunset, an edifice toppling
in broken masonry. The deluge.

Gondolas prowl through lagoons
between palaces that already sag,
their tapestry mildewed and flaked
like those ramshackle fallacies of hope.

II

Soured and gout-worn, he hid
from green calumny, dismayed by men,
by steam and speed slicing through nature.
Disgust drove him deeper into his hole.

It seemed as if life itself
was only a space to cram
the red and golden blaze of paint
across those distant horizons.

Like a haunting outside the frame
of day, the images from history
darken and clamp. For a moment the light
splinters, usurped by drumcloud.

Still he pieced that concept of something
lost and beyond us, a splash and streak
of sun and water fusing, the huge
melancholy of shaping a vision.

What it cost built his rack
and achievement, that stuns us now
as we look. An explosive mixing of pigments
made a radiance of mystery.

Down to the very end he sealed
his meaning: 'You cannot ever
read me, and do not care. Let it all
pass; go your ways.'

And then as bent custom would have it,
they laid the painter in St Paul's —
one skull that had seen the pure value of light,
the fleeting whirlwind of light . . .

Testimony

Democracy
is a rattle on the doorstep
at seven in the morning
and you know it's the milkman.

One Sunday we were sleeping with our wives
when who should rap on the door
but the secret police from Shrewsbury.
We refused to talk to them in English
so they went to Bala for handcuffs
and two interpreters.
We cooked them a breakfast of eggs
and sat around the kitchen in silence.
I gave one of them a copy of the Bible (in Welsh)
and he handed me a union jack.
They charged us at noon with sedition
and drove us to Swansea gaol.

As I write my memoirs in a cell,
I think of arrest and trial,
the rational portion of law
and the democratic process.
I wish we could find isolation,
dignified peasants without a Tsar.
                          Like the Russians
vilified and huddled together,
making our own mistakes,
giving two cold fingers to the world.

Where the Rainbow Ends

(Gilfach Goch, 26 March, 1974: for Sam)

My companion points to his cradle
in this gutted bowl of moorland scrub,
the slopes bravely greened
           and won from the black alps.
A crater tombstone a community,
        its heart ripped out.
My mind's eye sees his father
lift again from shallow pitwater
for the climb home, the thick black tea
and cheese, the cold eating him.

It is a blue spring dusk
as we enter the terraced loop
        above the gutted place.
The scooped past lies at our bootcaps,
and our people and their ways
gone with it.
        Down the valley
the stack-flares shoot like blowtorches,
the rattle of panic output
pricing men back into the market.

In the brittle kick of a moment's
accomplishment — this mind I sell for money —
nothing acts like the valleys' balance.
Away from the rickety cardboard struts
I feel a slider, diminished always
by yesterday's story. What dreams of kin
broke here beneath the ash? Nice sentiment
wears a lid, and gentility vanishes
with the layers of charm and grace.

120

My companion looks at the bedrock
of his nurture, the running hopes
of his beginning, on the sheeptrack mountain
        that once belonged to him
where tomorrow blew free as the wind.

Too old to forget, too proud
of stiff lineage to disown it,
we follow the bramble and rusted wire
out of yesterday — back to our customs
in the empty warmth that smothers
        what we have lost.

Commitment

Through a long fallow month, I could envy
the love-men, naturalists, land-
scapers, and diggers for old bones.

This chronicle I did not choose
stays tardy, and fails to give up another
missing piece. I sink to a dabbler.

The blinds are drawn, and the rain
spatters on the glass as I fiddle
with an elegy. That step I know so well

will not be heard tonight. To this
I have grown accustomed, yet linger
as if keeping vigil. So be it.

Capital

This will be the last ditch to fall
to the swing of its country.
Significance blowing down the hills
dies on the wind. Here the puffed
clink in their chains of office,
and the hagglers squat like a junta.

It is still as separate as an arm
lopped from its body: a strange sleeve
of territory spilled across the border.
What time has so carelessly mixed
clots here, where the ideals sag
and roots sprout only on the surface.

As long as I remember, the droll warmth
of its people has blurred
when our flag is lifted. Mouths are stitched.
Nothing is put to close scrutiny;
a knotted topic is flicked
into the bin, with a grin for Wales.

But now, in the distance, I think I hear
the young villagers build our future,
laying the first bricks of change.
This capital means less to them
than the land, where everything stems.
'Wait,' they are saying. 'Wait for us.'

A Kind of Penance

Unscraping to an ermine clique,
none of my kin brushed a catafalque
with soldiers bowed at the corners
and crowds to pay homage.

Swinging knapsacks to a shaft
they booted it, some bandily from a stoop
in a low steam. Unlike the film
they never sang on the road to the pit.

Near forty years on, their waste
sticks like a burr to my spirit
and will not loosen. Uncharity
drifts even to friends. Who are these

I watch now at the soft coffee-hour,
seeming all-in-all to themselves?
We are padded through the kind hours
at such distance from our crippled stock.

Unfair, the dealer's haphazard spray
that sends men to deep dark
and others capering in light.
Their portion of history drums at the mind.

Loss shrivels enterprise to a dot:
some things I latched to significance
— dignity and worth beyond price —
slip their eminence and become like the dead.

One day, clear as a black marker,
the lost ghost that relates to nothing
must show itself. All those deaths
shape my own defeat. It is inescapable.

Bards

In places where the language is spoken
   they dissolve into the people,
asking for no pompous rank
   or red carpet to their doors.
Sometimes a cap is doffed
   to one who has reached an eminence
of years and chairs of honour.
   I remember an old lady who said:
'I see Mr Llewelyn has died.
   I didn't know he was a poet.'
Fame for them is a tarnished bauble at best.

   Parson, teacher, tailor, clerk,
in rooms with the candles guttering
   they wrote what they felt and saw
on pages that may always be lost
   to the outside world. Yet there are two
or three who would hold their skill
   with Europe's paragons.
For more than a thousand years
   their role has not changed,
nor would they wish it to plant them
   apart from their fertile soil.

The Captain's Visit

(I.M. David Jones, d.28.X.74)

Stand easy, men. I see all your brasses are
shiny, and your webbing clean, and your
boots. Sergeant, give them a tot before I
commence. Tell your lance-jack to pour a
good slug, and top up that brazier. Then
get him to mend my axle-pin.

Men, I come not to nag, or scold, like some
cook to her scullions. I am just here to put
you in the picture, as the redtabs say. I
know you think my job is to pry, like a
cardinal's spy in a gaggle of priests. Not so.
I am subtler than that, having learned a
few tricks from my Celtic grandad.

This thing we have in hand now, this small
matter that must have blown to you on the
wind. You think it gossip croaked by
village hags? Come now. You are field-
soldiers far from home, not bumpkin
dreamers lost in a cloud. I observe your
proud regimental flash, your campaign
ribbons, the bars for valour, and wound-
stripes. You are a brotherhood that bends
to discipline and rank and the habit of
command, ready to march at a pistol-shot.
In our various ways, we all serve
contemporary fact.

What is that fact? It is the fact of empire,
men, an empire's survival, nothing less.
Yes, warm your mittens there, take
another tot. In this province we are put to
this matter, this small affair to keep our
empire intact. Always remember that one
thin slit can bring dismemberment. Any
pallid heretic, any vile miscreant, any
turncoat presuming difference, who would
opt for demarcation or seed a black doubt,
must wither at our touch. Do I make
myself clear?

Corporal, distribute some cheese. Men,
tonight brew up, wet your whistles, swill
your pay on a binge with your mates, lift a
full jar in the barrack-canteen, burrow
beneath the shifts of the wenches. Then hit
your bunks at lights-out. But do not droop
maudlin at the rumour

of the horror of this thing

we do tomorrow. Put more charcoal on
that brazier, corporal. You are not tardy
conscipts or curdled milksops that shrink
from duty, so do not be pummelled or
doped by sick propaganda. We are the
infallible governing power, supreme in
dominion, we have behind us a phalanx of
steel. A double-issue of rum in the

morning, sergeant, keep a crisp eye open
for dissidents, take plenty of spades, dig
deep, and see the carpenter about the box.
Look men! I munch my cheese with you,
lift my cup, knowing you will acquit
yourselves splendidly at dawn.

That's all for now, sergeant. See to it.

This piece — unfixed in time — is loosely, and very modestly,
based on the idea of the commanding officer's address to
Roman troops in 'The Tribune's Visitation' — without
showing the split which was present in the tribune's own
emotions. I have also attempted to catch a whiff of its humour,
for the author was not solemn.

Epitaph at Gilfach Goch

I

Duffled against a knuckleduster wind
I crouch by the last rusted tram
tilted on a bank of tussock;
a drift of March snow
caps the eternal mountain;
two boys fly by on shag ponies
flicking their rope switches.
  Clear across the gap
like a skeleton of dead merriment
is the shell of the Six Bells.

This ripped hollow brings me back
as in some haunting — a tarted grave
where the well-meaning fumbled.
        There
the Britannic thundered, a frail thatch
of green lidding its scar;
under my boots lie the rich
thick districts of coal, now seamed forever.
Across the scoop, thin grass thrusts from slag
  above a fake waterfall,
rock culverts taming the stream
  of its old wildness.
Vandals in the boredom of static
struck at one eyeless chapel . . .
the high wheels and engine-sheds,
tramway and winding-house
gone for scrap . . .

II

Men, in their blue-print wisdom
came here with explosive estimates,
heavy gear and miles of pipe;
slabs, brick, fence, saplings,
trucks of seed for the slopes
to sculpt a park from a battlefield,
to build a haven in the waste.
A dawn-to-dusk 'dozer fleet
moved the screen of black alps from the bed.

They worked for some just benevolence,
a soft canopy over the past;
errors of reckless men
would be corrected, the price of dust
atoned, proof of revival soon given
to a dead rut. 'See,' the slide-rulers said.
'Observe what we have done. We have mended
your devastated cup. It is a lovely
    green Eden we have shaped.'

III

Who dares jib at such noble motive
in this desolate garden they have left,
like a skull with bluebells in its sockets?
How could they know of the pumpless heart?
    The bustling past is locked
only in the memory of a dwindling few
mulled on vestiges of warmth;
they inherit a shuttered plot,

the commune of ghosts.
All that moneyed skill, the dream and wine
of the landscaper, ends here in a gutted void.
Severed pocket, once thriving to the rhythm
of its shifts, dies slowly on a soulless rim.
                         Beyond this rusted tram
and fleece-hung wire, tangled bramble in scrub —
beyond the broken, blasted, footworn moor
and the fox's home, there is only a Senghenydd
silence, and the old companion of wind
                         huddling its people . . .

Iolo Goch

Laureate at court, that fulsome trumpet
for your volatile lord in heroic mould
sets my teeth on edge. But how you blew!
At moated Sycharth, his wooden house with tiles
four-pillared on a green hill
you splashed praise across the groaning
table, high among bards.
You worshipped almost to frenzy
your clever, valiant, affable
          and bountiful patron
who stopped two kings and twelve armies.
You were knotted to him, this prince
once to appear and never again.

Then, dropped in the great empty
torchlit halls, you saw the dream
depart, leaving only a trace in the mind.
You sat by the ashes and wept
for the lost eagle of Cambria.
Like that brief streaking comet
he lit the front of heaven.

Letter to Captain Thwaite

Sir, begging your pardon
and allowing for your hectic business
at this rushing time,
but if you could see your road
clear to relieving me from my soldier
and religion oath, I would be much obliged
if you could release me for home now, and back
to my farm in Radnor. I do not intend
to complain, but at rough Naseby
where I fought in the VII Horse under Col Rich
I saw sufficient slaughter
to pock me with simple doubt
as to our presence there
to lift Christ up. He did not appear
to be anywhere in the centre
of that carnage. For truth, I did not know
the difference between them and us. I am not
a clever man, but I trust you will see
what I mean. Hoping very much you may consider
my proper request, sir.

Irony

Without Welsh, there are towns
here I don't enter.
I am thinking of those
who must preserve it;
they should speak nothing else
when the interloper fumes
at the ways of the barbaric.

That girl in the college
was right: who am I
to pronounce, going stripped
through my own land?
I liked her red venom.

(In five minutes, who could tell
of a view of the sea,
the sun going down
on a bare landscape —
the falls at Torpantau,
the blue distances of Gower?
All I need, then, is silence).

Think. One day this dry
English pen, this arrogant
instrument, will no longer
be required. Then my short
modest task will be done.

Catholics

I

It is a long way from their high
trappings of baroque. Inside this cramped
bramble'd shell, a splinter of history
reveals itself: more tangible
than broken arch and clamping ivy,
a few peasants bend in prayer
stumbling through Latin, rooted
to an outpost of a pummelled faith.
      I try to see the fourteen stations
on a wall, and the people making
a cross in the air. But it fades.

II

There were pockets of them
along the border — a random scattering
screened from Calvin and salvation,
just in touch with their monks.
               Under the Black
Mountains, huddled into cold
hollows, into stone boxes
like this, what could they hold
in common with Rome's pomp?
Did the signals of bishops,
the truth of a remote Pope
leak through to these hamlets?
Did they know a cardinal's hat
or the flock under a balcony?
They saw nothing of marble vastness
that needed a hundred cleaners,
or desks where religious clerks

checked the credentials of sainthood.
Perhaps a priest landed from the Irish
packet, flicking a skeleton gig
to bring news of papal bulls.

III

It is another forgotten heap
buried in deep woods, hidden
by thornscrub. How often
along a ridge, in copses of blown
stump, or on outcrops of fern
we see these remnants of floor
and wall, mysterious, unmapped —
rooms that concealed the hook of God.

I climb out of the undergrowth,
burrs clinging to my cardigan,
boots sucked into shallow marsh
before I jump a brook on logs
and find the old cattle track.

        Everything
seems too distant from surety,
from devoutness by candlelight
and the burning incense of ceremony
through those clockwork rituals.
    Bereft of credence, murky doubt
is all I can feel, the banality
of emptiness.
           They
clinched to some fuller splendour
than this, where a few dim

seasons of life were soon done.
Yet pity stirs me, for the simple fact
of their vanishing, for the end of them
here.

Summer '76

(for Jean)

We, sodden at the wet latitudes
who were born with rain slapping the window
dripped sweat in a heat-sump
where sheep cropped on reservoir beds,
still rivers turned green
and black scum floated on top
reeking enough to scare off the birds.
    Cold water was kept like wine
    in ewers in the larder dark.

The garden died with its lawns
dry as shredded wheat; even the weeds
gave up, and apples drummed all day
on the burnt grass.

        I could not concentrate
except on the ecstasy of lime-juice,
the bliss of ice-cubes to parched lips —
being stunned by heat, doing things at a slug's
quarter-speed, hating the stuck keys
of my typewriter, noting the boredom
of words when the sun began to show
its mettle, stopping the ballpoint
in my fingers.
        I looked again, through tinted lenses,
at that masterpiece of a sun —
the blazing Venetian disc that Turner worshippe
the perfect orange roundness
    slipping down behind roofs and trees
when it's day's fury was done.

I could respect
its ferocity, its terrible ability to shrivel us
like weeds . . .

Castle

On the tour the old guide showed us
the great banqueting hall where they feasted
off huge chops, swan, venison, brandy wine;
and the bedrooms where they enjoyed incest,
breeding simpletons to keep it in the family
and a name on the enormous maps.
    A priest was kept at the back
    on a pallet and ration of wine
    to bless killers off to Jerusalem.

Then we saw the dungeons' slimed walls
with rack, screws, brazier and rusted manacles
where they cut off tongues and put out eyes.
    When kings held a Christmas court,
the baying of hounds and the squawking of chickens
blotted out the screams from downstairs.

It was all log-fires then —
wood, stone, leather, hide and sheepskin
in turrets of fatal draught, the women tough as boots
through marriages of freezing utility.

The guide didn't mention the smells and disease,
or the rats, the battalions of cockroaches.
    Or the intelligence
of corkscrew lords, devious in the bone.
Or the dark and endless boredom
when those lovely, tall, fat, twelve-day candles
        red-numeral-marked in sections
        night by night sank into their wax . . .

Conditions of Pain

At dusk my father brought a sparrow in.
One of its eyes was a blob of blood
caught on a thorn or slashed
by some cat. We put it in the greenhouse
with crumbs and a saucer of milk.
All we could do. But it was dead before dawn.

In Cardiff Market on the fish stall
there was this poor lobster
with its jaws tied by elastic
crawling over rocks in a glass case.
People looked at the lobster with curiosity
or fascination, as it blundered about.

I knew a tomcat in Westfield
so old it could hardly walk,
wheezing towards me for a stroke.
Day and night on a front doorstep
in cold and rain, dying in his yellow
sick eyes, wanting something to end.

In New Quay behind the Black Lion
a forgotten donkey stared back at me
from its barbed-wire patch without grass.
And on the screen inside the pub
a young seal was being clubbed to death
as it looked up at horror on the ice.

Images of pain, fragments of suffering
stored in my memory until I die.
Oh God, I say to myself, instinctively
for there is no one else to appeal to
as these things continue, everywhere, all the time.
Compassion goes beyond compassion, and into pain.

from

FOR KING AND COUNTRY

Dering Lines '45

1

He was my first sight of evil,
a masterpiece of cunning:
Sergeant Hopkin, blonde as an actress
with small pig eyes like blue ice,
marched us up to the butts
to pick mushrooms for his mess.
I tried to pick toadstools, but was afraid.
Then we'd lie flat on the turf and click triggers
at invisible planes. Rifle Ack-Ack they called it.

'You, come here' said Hopkin, jabbing a finger.
'You're shooting like a frog
at those bloody Messerschmitts.'
His red lips were always moist,
he kept sliding his tongue around them
while his poor brain flamed and would one day break
on its path to insanity.

2

Dead sheep littered the ranges
burst open by grenades, and farmers cursed in Welsh
as we trudged through their cattle pancakes.
The skulls of the poor sheep were everywhere.

Summer rain screened the Lines
sunk deep in raw country,
boots crunched on concrete
in our trap in the hills.
We wiped guns and shone brass,

bending to sadists with stripes on their sleeves:
    'You're a fuckin shower. You're frogs. Wot are you?'
    'Frogs, sergeant.'

Boredom was worn like a second skin
as we darned socks and sewed buttons,
whitewashed the cokeshed, saluted anything that moved;
once, six of us hacked a lawn with knives.
    We slept on pallets where beetles lived
inside the straw, snug in the warm.
We were a mix of bully-boys from the ports
and callow bundles of shock from Ebenezer.

Our mentors were old sweats:
brave Rats who fought Rommel
now cynical and venomous, growling for their tickets.
    Here the crack Welsh regiments of the line
    with the skulls of Rorke's Drift in their cupboards
    ran down to a skivy remnant.

I was young, respectable as a curate,
flummoxed by foul language and strapped
inside my Baptist straitjacket.
    There I learnt to drink draught Bass,
    jig with fast Naafi girls
    and fritter my lean 19th year
among the reek of latrines and bolt-oil
in the bleak scooped uplands of Epynt.

Burial Party

Probert told me. The lieutenant was blown
to bits on the grenade range
looking for a dud. 'Jesus
it was a fuckin mess,' Probert said.

Poplars dripped. The box draped with a Jack
was lifted off the wet gun-carriage;
the bearers almost dropped it
as one of them slid in the slime.

Four of us had dug a hole in a copse
on a slope not far from their house.
Our capes were soaked, our boots were caked.
There was this drizzle, continuous, and much
slithering about in mud as the box
was lowered. The widow's black stockings
were splashed with mud. Buglers lined up and blew
a short Last Post — piercing and eardrum-banging
on the dawn air. Riflemen discharged their blanks
as the little knot of mourners
waited for the thing to end.

We covered him up, flattened out the earth,
slung spades and rakes on a jeep,
lit cigarettes and sludged back in the rain
through the sopping Breconshire fields.

'I'm going to get pissed tonight'
said Probert. Pity was a four-letter word
we never used, and all I could feel
was an emptiness, the beginning of pity.

Pay Detachment, Exeter

This was where the dregs went
down to the bottom of the barrel
when the regiments spewed them out.
We had bad feet, squints, glass eyes, unhappy childhoods
and the look of rodneys on the run.
But we could add up shillings and pence,
write vouchers to destitute wives
when their men scarpered. We played cards
and drank applejack from the farms.

I knew then
none of us would enter the Ministry
or speak to the Cymmrodorion.
We were not
the 20th Valeria Victrix, proud under Trajan,
defending the western limits of empire.

We were what our time had made us
coming in at the end of a war:
small, insignificant, and wary
of speeches and flags.

'Taurus Intelligentsia Frustrat'
(Bullshit baffles the mind)
was our motto in pidgin-Latin
over the door of the bogs.

from
PASSING THROUGH

Walnut Tree Forge

My father shod horses in the sun
while I threw old shoes at an iron pin.
From the bank of the canal I saw
a kingfisher dive like a blue-green streak
clean through the water and out again
with lunch in its beak, then glide
to its fish-boned hole in the bank.

My father would look up from his work
and lean against the door to rest
from the bending, the weight on his back
of a shire, big and restless in the heat,
that tested all his muscles and skill.
He would wipe his brow with a rag.
'Did you see a kingfisher, then?' I nodded.

He never welcomed the big horses
made for show, all rump and heavy
with the spoilt pride of their runners,
shone to a tantrum and cockade gloss
for anything but work. These gave him
a rough hour of shifting and fret,
too pampered by the hands of others.

It was labour to him, one more task
for a pound, the ponies coming in a string
on a good day. To me it was freedom
from arithmetic, as golden time used up
so easily. There were just the two of us,
the ring of the shoes hitting the pin,
and a kingfisher, and a shire, in the long-ago sun.

Connection in Bridgend

In the bus café, drinking tea, I watch
nothing happening in Bridgend.
I mean, there is rain, some shoppers
under canopies, tyres sloshing them
from the gutters. Otherwise not much.

(Do those Pakistanis feel the cold?
What are they doing in Bridgend?
How did they land here, and those lost
Sikhs and Chinamen?
I am sorry for them, they look bereft.)

In the café a young mother is being given
stick by her two boys. They want Coke
and her baby cries for no reason
unless he's seen enough of Bridgend.
I feel an odd kinship with him.

At last my bacon sandwich is done;
it was something to look forward to,
slicing a minute's delight into the murk.
Balancing the plate, I hold the sad babe
while his mother fetches the Coke.

Then a one-armed paperseller comes in
with a strip of frayed ribbons on his coat.
He wants to tell me his story,
so I listen while the baby sobs
and his brothers suck straws.

An hour ago, I was alone; now
there are six. Even the café-owner
squeezes out a smile. We are in it
together, until the last buses go out.
One by one they leave the bays.

Good Friday

I purchase my small Easter offerings:
a Black Magic egg for my friend,
six hot cross buns for my father,
an uplift card to a pious aunt.
These are customary over the years
since the loss of our stiffer
rituals — the morning prayer, the fish
at dinner, the evening walk
with Bibles to the long sermon.

On the wind I hear the chimes
from Ararat, calling its remnant.
Another house opens at noon
packed with lapsed Christians
who drink swiftly against the clock
and stay on past the dead taps.
I fool myself into some pretence
of joy, pressing down a hollowness
and not knowing why it comes.

Hours go by. . . . I spend the whole day
watching a screen, reading old papers
and drinking tea. Then I put out
the milk bottle, and feed the cat.
Another Good Friday draws to a close,
tied completely to the temporal.
I switch off the lamps. As usual
there is something seriously missing,
but I do not know what it is.

Bitter Morsel

Together we burrowed above quadrangles,
digging out the perfidy of kings
and the tracks of feckless clerics
crawling in a slime of dominion.

History with its twists and dead ends,
its tardiness to yield the truth,
slowed our clocks in useless rummaging.
There was a lesson here, if we could learn it.

When she linked my fingers, I pondered
our own acts of treason, as we drop
into false alliances. Even my thought
formed like an essay, precise and detached.

Release from entrapment was the aim
to stop her ivy clinging, to pursue
sweet knowledge in some solitary drum
where the chaos was my own making.

Dalliance capered on, through a summer
of smoky functions awash with wine
and riddled with hurt. Communication
chopped itself down to silence.

'Goodbye then' at the train. I would come to know
the insignificance of kings and clerics
against the warmth of our couplings,
the blaze of the living moment.

Passing Through

I

Above the reservoir, my friend and I
picnic from a hamper like two provincials
in a French print. We watch
cherry sails on small boats
with little figures in them —
distant specks on calm water.

A solitary fishes from a skiff at the rim,
oblivious to the racers waiting for a breeze
on a June day of tropic heat,
of lemon light when the sun
warms us like some kind reward,
doing its duty at last.

Below on a wooded slope
a couple flick cakecrumbs to the birds
hopping close, domestic for a moment,
sharing this hour with us.
They come almost to the hand
competing for scraps in a free restaurant.

II

I absorb the scene, a fragment of harmony,
squinting through glasses at those far dots,
knowing it will never be repeated
exactly as it is today.
We try to preserve the cherished
but the sift of time dissolves it.

My friend, the endearment I feel for her
(especially now in her Venetian boater with a blue strip),
those red sails and small figures, the sun
spoiling us, the young couple
and the birds blend together
for a while, then pass . . .

It is not simply drift
but a severance too sudden, unlooked-for —
a thin wire of love soon snapped.
Even these images will crumble
as a poor reminder of this day —
transient, heartbreaking, gone . . .

Let me linger here above the reservoir
to keep something only for a minute,
to hold what passes like quicksilver,
I have an instinct to preserve
which seems to rely on loss.
It is the loss that is insupportable.

Armistice Day '77, Honiton

The two minutes' silence was cut to one
that November day; it was a busy world.
By chance, on my way to a gig,
I walked into a ceremony of six
in the rain: crosses in a ring, and the poppies soaked.

Down two sides of the slab were names
linked to this piece of England — the sound
of country stock grown old in duty
and the acceptance of pointless loss.
Names going back to Minden and before.

(Were these the only ones left
to remember their dead?
Already sixty seconds were lopped
off any dignity. Would their children
forget, as I had forgotten?)

No more came. On some other day
I might have felt an interloper
marring their ritual. At eleven o'clock
the men took off their hats
and we all bowed our heads.

A minute in the rain in a country town
may whisper the whole grief of history.
Picture a knot of seven around that block,
the red wet poppies, and for just a moment
a complete and utter silence in the world.

Twilight in the Library

I have not come within their frozen
North, but we all go there
sometime. The entry visa
is age and complete silence
broken only by pages turning.
On a wall is a fitting print
of old people drowsy in Salem.
It takes months of visits, scanning
curled copies of *Punch*
or *Harper's Bazaar*, to reserve your seat.

I offer the old men tobacco
for a roll; they accept me tardily
into the room. They take turns
to keep the tiers of racks tidy
and journals in their proper slots.
                              They trail
bleak lifetimes behind them . . .
and cough and cough. The Elder
has a red nose and silver stubble,
his magnifier races across *The Times*
and *Guardian*. He is the group's
intellectual, full of useless facts,
making notes in a secret pad
and scribbling faster as closing-time comes.

Rain drips down the sooted panes.
The Elder wheezes over a magazine
while his cronies grunt and sleep, creaking
into December, warming themselves
against hot pipes, propped at the long tables.

There is a sense of all the days ending,
a reluctance to face the night
as the lights come on in the precinct
and a keeper points to the clock.

UNCOLLECTED AND UNPUBLISHED

Henry Signs

The blaze of gold quartering
is caught in a sun flood through the high window
    flashing all ways at once.
Ancestors slabbed in marble on the walls,
    pearl, brocade and scarlet lions
jumping in the lemon shafts.
    The living Holbein portrait hoists
himself and his precious cod-piece
    off his ulcered calves,
thinking of bed and backgammon.
    Lee and Cromwell and a creep of courtiers,
a slither of damp bishops
    ease to the long table.
The pale black secretary dips the quill
    and hands it to the ruin:
this once Golden Hope of the New Learning
    soon to queen again
as easy as he split from Rome,
    and now with levity pocketing
the hapless land to the west.
    Sun-slant catches his enormous
ring-seal as he lifts his ruffed whiskers,
    shakes white lawn sleeves
back from his wrists, scratches slowly
    on buff parchment, and impresses red wax
with the ring, screwing it left and right
    thoroughly for four hundred years.

from No Man's Land

Morning

The mirror reflects evidence
of time, a story almost formed.
You are still several persons
and cannot settle for whatever
you've become. When the setting
seems right, you play the clown;
when the philosophers come
you may open a box of tricks
with an insight here, an apt quote
there, the brow thought-furrowed.
A jester crouches within you
and juggles for the shallow court;
the axe-man behind him
puckers a cynical mouth.

Some blunt giggling understudy
always capers from the wings
to take over your sagging Hamlet —
that family paragon who has slummed
through a mile of gutters.

There is really no celebration
in this glass. Only two blank eyes
dead in their sockets.

Leaf from a Log-book

It is March the 5th. The weathercocks creak on their
      swivels
as the sea wind bangs in.
It has been like this for a month now.
It is lonely now, the women keep breaking
and the children are in poor shape.
The first sign of oddness was the absence
of the postman from the town
after about a week.
No cars came down the lanes,
the telephone was out of order
and the wireless went dead.
We watched a tanker passing
out to sea, her decks were deserted
and two days later a plane
dived into the sea.
There was no noise
and no warning. I said to my wife,
you know what this is? (The thing that stacked up
for thirty years elsewhere
has occurred elsewhere.)

There are plenty of vegetables on the smallholding
and our single neighbour has a pig and a cow
(slow catastrophe he calls it).
There are tins in the larder
and fresh water from a spring.
We can last about three months
in the accustomed way, apart from this silence.

If this is the end, it is not coming quickly
or violently. Some fools and strangers somewhere else
have cooked this up for us . . .

Bourgeois Evening

You see that man there? The one
    clarifying some obscurity of commerce
as he palms a balloon-glass of cognac?
    For him, the last of mystique disappeared
with Churchill, golf is the panacea,
    communism squats in beard and corduroy
and Vietnam is a seven-lettered word.
    He is dying after a thousand years.

Who dares disturb his riffling
    of fivers? Two generations
of banditry in affluent twilight
    will see his philosophy through
in Surrey pineland and shuttered club
    unless blinkers bring their own price
when the pilots zoom to stardom
    and the brandy cracks in his hand.

Winter, 1968, St John's Wood

This morning, in the mirror, I saw the face
of a man on the run.
I am still single, highly-strung
and not receiving my quota.
On Sundays I sit in Paddington
and eat girls with my eyes.
Midnight orgies flop on endless speech.
I live in a city where the fog throws
a quilt over the roofs —
even the pigeons can't sight
the garbage cans. The crows fly very low.
I grope for the orange juice.
Through the window I squint at the murk
as transistors spew out the jockeys.
Outside, an Irishman kicks the starter
of a pneumatic drill. He's been there for days
breaking up the pavement.
On the stair there's a smell of cat.
A week's mail lies on the tiles.
I balance a platter of sliding eggs
and two wafers of burnt hovis
on the mantelpiece.
The cheese grows blue in the ice-box,
the milk is a fungus junket,
the shredded wheat dries to a cake,
and my wilkinson swords
are rusting in the bathroom.
There and then I decide to quit,
go west to the place in the photograph.

In the patio at home,
father is puffing a pipe.
Sparrows cheep shreds in the silence.

Kindness and reason prevail.
In summer a shock orange sunball
shatters the trellis.

The Black Dog

Sometimes I fear it
    even now when it has gone.
It loped at the back,
    silent, waiting.

When joy was on the wind
    I could sense it lurk;
when youth ate the daylight
    I felt its shadow.

A brave man beats it
    away, or sees the fangs
are muzzled. He will tie
    a steel leash on it.

One day in bright sun
    who expected the thing
to reappear? I had planned
    a short break at the fair

without spectre or phantom —
    a feast of affection.
I had hoarded my ration
    of peace, of calm.

Then, edged at my vision,
    the black shape loped;
a cloud slid down the side
    of the green hill.

There were no shutters
    to hide behind. I had
no choice but to face it.
    Decaying breath fanned me

as I stared, paralysed
    in stone, its burning eyes
fixed. I stared, gaze locked.
    It shuffled, eyes cast down,

slowly turned and retreated.
    The cloud lifted as I shook,
not feeling a victor.
    Not feeling anything.

I continue to hope
    it will never return.
I occupy the loose hours
    reducing its dark shape.

For Cymru, These . . . .

The wine we have made for you
does not travel, it cannot cross
the border in these old casks.
Elsewhere they purchase the wine
that tastes like sudden sheepdip.
They are not, and never will be
acquainted with your excellence.

Down here in the coldest vault
I test your unchanging vintage
in the cobweb racks of centuries.
From long back, in another time,
some of the casks are cracked
and their essence dribbles red.
Tomorrow, tomorrow we shall mend them.

Father

If you should come to our silent
bungalow, he will either be potting
in the greenhouse, or mending something.
A clock, for instance. Our place
is full of timepieces, resurrected
from scrap. These tick and chime
all night, keeping guests awake.
I see his white head bend
over tomato plants, his fingers pick
with a penknife at a flywheel
in the littered shed. Then later
he cooks for us, a folded Cornish
pasty, seeping nourishment.
He is supreme at baking cake.

There were dark calamitous months
he lived through, the widower's
grieved adjustment to emptiness
after forty years. 'I preferred
the Somme,' he said to me.
She was as close to his side
as a woman could be, an exact
counterpart of a true maker,
destroying nothing. And now
in his late evening I see
all that I had missed before:
the calm, the patience, the kindness,
the country simplicity he wears,
that I will not inherit.

On Trying to Write a Love Poem

To Jeannie

I tried in four different houses
To write a poem of love.
In the Horse & Groom, the Upper Boat,
The Narrow Gauge, and the Turtle Dove,

I had a biro and a notebook
And images inside my head.
All the best moments together,
All the good things we'd shared.

Sitting in snugs and alcoves
I struggled with the sweetest theme
Of which John Donne was a master
And Dafydd ap Gwilym wrote reams.

But getting it right was harder
Than finding a pub on the map.
Nothing poured forth to inspire me
Except more bitter from the tap.

What could compete with reality,
An affection honest as bread?
I bought a little love-spoon in Brecon
And I gave her that instead.

Lines for J

I have met them:

the puffed politician, his ego bouncing ahead of him,
    listening to no one;
the clever architect without imagination,
    designing further enormity;
the slippery bureaucrat, eager
    to pulverise a landscape;
the tough journalist hunting a story,
    untouched by private life;
the hollow actor scribbling autographs,
    kissing himself in the mirror;
the spoilt poet, flattered by sycophants,
    unable to utter the truth;
the brittle women, painted in layers,
    their voices shrill as fishwives;
the selfish, whose selfishness
    has turned them into bores.

And you
who are none of these things,
but closer to nature than anyone I know;
who somehow takes the harshness out of life
    as if it were a gift.

Cricket at the National Library

'Pitch it up!' the captain said
as I trundled to the crease:
'Stop bowling bumpers.'
What he wanted was a loss
of speed, more slow left-arm
spin. I tried to oblige
but the language cherry reared up
again, wide of the off-stump.
'No ball' the umpire muttered.

I got more shine on it,
judged angle of flight and the in-
swing, curved it as a crafty
concealed googly. The atmosphere was quite
heavy, good for medium pace as I sent it
scattering the bails half-way
to the sight screen. My mind ached
from the effort. 'That's better,'
the captain said. 'You're coming on.'

The Complaint

(after reading R.S. Thomas's poem 'The Need')

Oh, I know them too: parsons, for instance,
Carpenters in verse, but above it all
High in their northern nests;
Skilled at chilly correspondence,
Cursing the taint of England
And the droop of the Welsh sun,
Remembering to send a lean book
Each year to their alien publisher, to collect
A fee from the smart magazine.
Do they grapple with their God
As Hopkins did, or chisel in vanity
Like us, for a silly chance
Of immortality? Sometimes I think
We are pride right through to the bone.

And who among us burst
A single grenade on England?
We need this long wallow
In the funeral of Wales.

They speak of 'Love of the land',
Have they ever scratched from dawn till dusk
Like a Merioneth peasant?
Not for them the devastated south
And its poets who have wept
For their dead. Vision and love
Will not bring my people back —
Those whose lungs were clogged
For distant profit.
Come down here, my preacher,
See the elegant cemeteries of the Rhondda Valley.
Better to die in an open field
Under your God's sun
Than like a rat in darkness.

The Lost Girls

     In Vaynor churchyard
where the nettle has drowned generations,
there is a slab inside rusty railings
with a Crawshay ironmaster beneath it.
Cut into the granite are the words
     GOD FORGIVE ME

Remorse too late, as always?
Rumours come down to Pontsarn and Vaynor
from such distance, of village girls
as maids and skivvies up in the castle
required to do certain 'things'.

Historians scoffed, but the villagers
did not, even now when their moral squint
               takes in Cyfartha.

I could picture it, in dark corners
of the wings and turrets of that house:
mottled hands fumbling at a bodice,
undoing buttons, lifting a starched
apron and skirt to forage and explore.
If the girl resisted, she was finished.
Down in the hovels they knew
what went on, those masters with a choice
of flesh before breakfast or luncheon
               and after dinner.
Insensitivity grew like fungus.

'Blow out the candle' one would command
as he moved some girl through curtains
and promised her promotion to lady's maid,
the thrust of an empire behind him,
the confidence of rich stags.

(Perhaps there was a single forerunner
proud and ahead of her time
who waited for the sweating grunting ram
to mount, to splay
open her legs, then she drew
a potato-knife from her apron pocket
and stabbed him in the rump.)

Someone's remorse made him tell the mason
to cut GOD FORGIVE ME on his slab
for the years of conscripted sex.

But from Georgetown through Dowlais to Vaynor,
nobody can find the graves
of the servant girls.

Photographs of Ourselves

Seen from above
it is blue and really round
with the coasts of continents outlined
as accurately as the geographers once fixed them,
floating in cold silent space
                    forever. . . .

And we are riding on it.
Beyond the parallels and hemispheres,
Jerusalem, Moscow and Rome,
Christ and Marx and the Pope
and our butcher's minute of history,
out into the cold spaces and beyond infinity,
there is nothing like us.
All the evidence of the instruments,
all the learned astronomers
confirm we are alone.
Alone with the rifle and machine-gun
and the blueprints of the doomsday weapon.
There is nowhere else for us to go
in the vast cold eternal silence.

It is our international loneliness.
I look up from England at the blue spaces, at the emptiness,
And feel like an ant in a pavement crack.
On this solitary spinning miracle
we are all we've got.

Life under Thatcher

Memories of Winter

1. Waste in Astey's

They sit all over the café
not waiting for buses
but just sitting there
murdering time — empty cups
and hours before them.
Quiet, alone, from 16 to 60
and beyond. I drink my warm soup
quickly, and leave the cold place.
A glimpse inside my wallet confirms
I will not eat at the Mandarin.

In Astey's you can see a recession
at work. Outside, it looks like New York
on the pavements: fried chicken cartons
and crushed Coke cans, the garbage
of the West.
          I live in a country
          like the crummy kitchen
          behind a posh restaurant,
          the cockroaches the customers
          never see.
                    Something festers here,
                    a bowl of rotting cherries
                    where the rainbow ends.

2. Tension exposed

'You're always under my feet'
his wife said. Then she turned
to the camera: 'He's always
under my feet' she groused.
Her husband looked as if
she had just hit him; a slap
on the face would be better
than this . . . nothingness.
'I go down to the club' he said
'and play cards, have a jar.
Sometimes I walk along the sands.
A few have already jumped off
the cliffs down there.
I'm not saying unemployment's
to blame.' He wasn't saying it
but you could see he thought it.
They both fondled their tot
who cried and cried.
'We get in each other's way'
his wife said, not letting up.
She had her job to do
about the house, but he'd lost his.

I couldn't watch any more,
his dignity ebbing away,
she falling to pieces
on television, before millions.

3. On Hayes Island

Young miners down for the day
sit apart, huddled like a cabal;
for some reason they remind me
of those Red sailors who mutinied
long ago.
         Under a gunmetal sky
the pigeons gather for crumbs
as I freeze at a tin table
above the public convenience,
waiting for something to turn up,
feeling far from debonair
in the black ice of a scimitar winter.

This is Cardiff's Montmartre
without the wine and conversation.
You can buy wine from a store
and drink it unmolested on a bench,
but you can't buy conversation.
It is a rendezvous for the impoverished
pockets of want that dwell on the brink.

Listless, I tap my shoe
on the bottle-glass grid of the bog roof
and watch the fine women of South Wales
shuttling across the Hayes.
They look as if they're going somewhere,
serious, with bulging shopping bags.

At dusk, the clock on St John's Church
strikes five as a drizzle begins
and the shutters go up on the tea shack.
By now, even the pigeons have had enough
and fly away to Splott . . .

4. Slender means

Convoys of coke lorries hogged the M4.
Vans full of bluebottles came back from the picket lines.
Wales was being fucked-up again.

The poetry workshop was inside a shed
where the box was switched off
when the last channel died.
They were sprawled on a sofa with its stuffing
hanging out, and on the floor,
watching a repeat of some junk
when I came in, my visit covered
by the Gulbenkian Foundation. (Savour
the irony of such benevolence.)

A few young and older
waiting for culture in limbo.
        (Beckett seemed apt.)
One of them said they were fuelled
on chips, baked beans, sardines,
corned beef, apples and Pro-plus pills.
You couldn't get much pot in Resolven on benefits.
He pulled the tv-lead out of its wall socket
and we talked about Them and Us —
mostly Them in the Promised Land
where money sings.

5. Consumers

Losing my way in the hypermarket
I watched the solemn consumers
pushing heaped trolleys of food

down the aisles, as if stocking up
for their futures, or a nuclear winter.
A small fortune lit up the tills.
I thought of human wreckage in Astey's
and Caroline Street, the chilling misery.
At the checkout I paid for my treat —
a half-bottle of Tesco Scotch.
To keep up my pecker.

On every corner there's a bank
where people file up outside
to stick plastic cards into a wall.
Vandalised churches gape, their assemblies
dissolving into the secular supermarkets.

On Monday my father draws his pension
to consume as little as possible.
On Thursdays I meet cronies from the dole line
who are not big spenders.
We spoon faggots-and-peas on the market balcony.

Journalists call it despair
but it's controlled, like rage.
The unsaid things are often said
in other ways, through a silence
full of generosity, within circles
                    of fraternal warmth.

6. Sleeping quarters

Two ragamuffins were building a den
(like the ones we used to make as kids)
out of cardboard boxes, plastic bags, corrugated sheet,

foliage and planks, at the back
of a wrecked church in Charles Street
behind high trees, bushes, bramble, fences.
'Makin' a kip' one of them said.
It looked as if it might last the night
but not much longer. 'We got two more
in Canton and Fairwater'
as if these were palatial villas,
summer and winter residences for toffs.
'They look a bit makeshift' I said.
'There's no rent to pay' he said.
I left them to it, whistling away,
twin casualties of the economy
preparing for a cosy night
                              under the stars.

7. Roadhouse

The old man asks for free burnt crackling
off the cold pork, and is refused.
His crumbling sister, who's always here,
smiles and tilts her stout, while punters
stoop over the race-form, concentrating
with magnifiers like marshals over their maps.
Most read the *Sun*, some the *Mirror*.

Our village inn is now a Ploughman's Lunch,
a merchants' crevice, a horse-brass grub pit
for moneyturners from the town
that spawned these fat cats.
We deserve it: and these crows too
on the Common, flapping down outside the portholes
like some squadron of doom.

8. Gig

Where are we probing in this sleet
that falls like arrows?
The organiser is adrift
when I enter the Custom House
with flaking 'Hennessy' on the door;
then the vast Golden Cross
(tipped by Betjeman as a sample
of green marble glory for the proles)
with its whiff of life-at-the-bottom.
It is Cardiff's Eleanor Rigbyville
where the lonely pack like mackerel.

We link up as the wet night slumps,
sip bad plonk from paper cups
surrounded by paintings of oxtail soup
and lumps of meat out of Bacon.
We spout pieces in a loft of corridors,
a converted Victorian sweatshop
off Bute Street. The drum is haunted
by skeletons in long rows
hoping for a week they could get through
and pig's trotters on Sunday.

The knot of listeners loll about
like people waiting for a train
as we clock our obsessions.
I note a sign of the times:
poetry has let loose the ranters
who scream in a social mesh.

There is a mike but no chairs,
it's colder than Adamsdown in winter

when the fuses blow —
        and once again
I puzzle at the raving salvo of language,
    at the oddity of their aims.

9. Fragment

At a Greasy Spoon in Quay Street
I hear a woman saying to another:
'Be philosophical, don't think about it.'
'But I want to change my character'
comes the reply. The other woman
has no answer to this.

My coffee goes tepid as I ponder
that woman changing the character
she doesn't want, aided by her friend
who told her to be philosophical.

Then: 'No job, no money, and now he's gone.
It was the strike that did it.'
A whole chronicle opens up behind her.

Then her logical friend trots out a gem:
'We wouldn't worry what people think of us
if we knew how little they do.'

10. Bad night

Packs of vandals in alpine boots
      (built to kick heads in)
fester the streets: they maraud

like Barbarians outside Rome
or the last jackals
after Armageddon. You cannot
eat a curry in peace; the poor Indians
look scared, rarely penetrating
the centre after dark, where those steelcaps
are aimed at their genitals.
Immigrants could commit suicide at 2 a.m.
if they walked across the bridge to Riverside.

               Is this
the capital of Wales? It was never
Tunbridge Wells, but now it is perilous
to enter a ramshackle Gents
     at the wrong end of town
where booze-soaked punks lurk
to use their huge boots.
             If I quote
R.S. Thomas at them, they'll kick
          the shit out of me.
We should send them to Beirut
              or Eton.

Some strut on the sick wing
of the NF, and petrify
even Thatcher's backwoodsmen
sleeping under their union jacks
out in Lisvane.

Cursing blobs, immaculate in their way
of bleached denim and redneck braces,
they bludgeon from the warrens
of the estates, and prowl and boil through towns

like an invasion of violent farmhands
       for their fix of mayhem.

I doubt if they listen to Mozart, or read Orwell.
There's a reason for it. There always is.

The Return of Old Sandeman

On my 43rd birthday the stocktaker
returned. He looked the same
but was three years older. I thought,
he grows old too, the sly bastard.
His flat black Spanish hat was on a tilt
and he had a transistor under his cape,
making the noises of 1970. His stop-watch had a loud tick.
He carried a ciné camera. a bottle of Babycham
      and instructions for playing bingo.
I thought, he's no longer serious,
he's becoming one of us.
He had a Mini outside, a portable Japanese
      television set and two blondes.
The greedy sod, I thought,
he's been living it up for three years.

What have you got to report, he said.
Have you filled those pages yet?
A few, I said, I've covered many lines
with perishable verse, two weddings
      three funerals, four friendships
      and the love of my life.
I have tried to be oblique and reserved,
reticent to the point of vanishing,
but my barometer of sensitivity has cracked
and my mouth is an obsolete Bren gun.
On Aug 20, 1969, I helped an old lady across the road.

Good, he said. That's a nice report.
Now I would like to take some pictures
      of you, have a drink and play a
      round of bingo. You can have one
      of the blondes if you like.

I looked at him as he fidgeted with the clock.
What had I been afraid of?
He was only a lollipop, soon converted to the daft life.
Get out of my dusty room, I said,
and take your junk with you.
I will speak only to your superior.

He crept backwards through the door, muttering,
clutching his apparatus of frivolity.
Oddly enough, I felt sorry for him.